Praise for
SLAY THE MEETING

"Embark on a quest with two brave co-workers and their reluctant boss as they battle the dreaded Meeting Monster! This beast feeds on creativity and joy, leaving meetings lifeless. But fear not! This playful tale is packed with practical tips to vanquish the monster and triumph in online and hybrid meetings!"

—Keith McCandless,
Co-author, Liberating Structures

"Fun and practical, at times I felt like these characters were lifted from my own life. Many of us will be able to relate to the pains of poor meetings in these stories. But what sets it apart is the clear strategies and hands-on advice that can release us from the meeting monster. A truly unique take on a workplace practice that is long overdue to be turned on its head."

—Lizzie Benton,
Culture Coach, Liberty Mind Ltd.

"While many of us suffer from too many meetings, few of us know how to effectively get rid of them. This book solves that problem. Mun-Wai has gifted us with her expert, actionable advice for taking back our workdays, so we can focus on work that really matters."

—Joshua Kerievky,
CEO, Industrial Logic

"A delightful parable about how to eliminate unnecessary meetings and make the most of useful meetings. Read it and use it the next time you're considering calling a meeting or it's your turn to facilitate a meeting."

—Johanna Rothman,
Author, Modern Management Made Easy series

"'This meeting could have been an email.' How many times have we thought (or even said) this? In *Slay the Meeting Monster*, Mun-Wai empowers us to transform meetings from dreaded time-wasters into vibrant hubs of collaboration and innovation. This book is a must-read for anyone seeking to boost productivity, enhance team dynamics, and cultivate a healthier, more fulfilling work life."

—Evan Leybourn,
Co-founder, Business Agility Institute

"Great read! The storyline is much more enjoyable to read than a traditional 'business book' and is an effective way to convey the key points. It immediately motivates you to think about how to optimize meetings, schedules, and team interactions in general. Loved it!"

—Chris Boni,
SVP, New Media Games, Aristocrat

"I enjoyed reading the book. It is very well structured and easy to follow. The book addresses many of the pain points from meeting overload in today's work environment and suggests practical ways to alleviate the pain. The concept is easy to understand but yet these are those we easily miss out in a modern workplace."

—Marc Chan,
General Manager, RingCentral

SLAY
THE
MEETING
MONSTER

A Business Parable

Get Rid of Meetings
and Get More Done

Mun-Wai Chung

Paperback ISBN: 979-8-9920240-0-5
Ebook ISBN: 979-8-9920240-1-2

CONTENTS

ACKNOWLEDGMENTS

NO BOOK IS WRITTEN ALONE, and this one is no exception. My writing journey has been anything but solitary, and I owe a debt of gratitude to many who have offered their invaluable support.

First and foremost, a huge shout-out to JF Unson, who co-wrote all the blogs about meetings that laid the foundation of this book's rough manuscript. JF's insights and dedication were instrumental in shaping the initial draft. He even partnered with me to revise that draft, meticulously incorporating feedback from the first round of developmental editing. Thank you, JF, for your expertise and unwavering support! This book would not have been possible without you.

I am also immensely grateful to my incredible book team at The Writer's Ally. Their work in editing, design, and marketing transformed that rough manuscript into the polished work you hold in your hands today. They not only kept me on schedule but also created timelines that accommodated my demands and life's unexpected detours. Allyson Machate, Ginni Smith, Julie Haase, Emily Hitchcock, and Clair Fink, thank you for your patience and flexibility in bringing this project to fruition! Your creativity and keen insights have elevated this book to new heights.

Equally important were our beta readers whose generous contributions of time and thoughtful feedback provided fresh perspectives and helped refine the content. Your suggestions and corrections were invaluable in ensuring this book best serves its readers. Thank you for your critical role in this process!

Finally, I would like to express my sincere appreciation to the many individuals who, over the years, taught me various subjects that contributed to the creation of this book, such as psychological safety, remote work, Liberating Structures, facilitation skills, and more. Your knowledge and expertise allowed me to experiment and apply these concepts in my work environments, and the results of those experiments became part of the content of this book. Your teachings have had a lasting impact on my professional journey and this book.

Writing *Slay the Meeting Monster: Get Rid of Meetings and Get More Done* has been a collaborative endeavor, and I am humbled by the contributions of each individual who played a role in bringing it to life. As you read this book, know that it represents not just my efforts, but the collective wisdom and support of many dedicated professionals.

INTRODUCTION

EVER FEEL LIKE YOUR WORKDAY IS AN ENDLESS LOOP of meetings, leaving little time for actual work? Do you drag yourself to yet another meeting, only to realize you've zoned out, half listening while covertly checking emails? By the time you return to your desk, you barely remember why you met in the first place.

If you answered yes to either of those questions, you're not alone.

Drawing from decades of experience treading through the dynamic landscape of companies ranging from start-ups to global enterprises and government/military contracts to the commercial sector, I've navigated the harsh reality of today's pervasive meeting culture—a phenomenon I like to call Death by a Thousand Meetings. In this professional landscape, we often find ourselves inundated with countless appointments that fall short of their intended impact. Yet we accept the invitation out of obligation, fear of missing out (FOMO), or the lack of a viable alternative. We become entangled in a cycle of meetings about meetings, where the act of gathering often takes up valuable productive time. Some professionals even turn these invites into a dubious status symbol, a misguided sense of self-importance rather than contributing genuine value. It's time for a collective wake-up call!

If you're ready to challenge the status quo, this book is for you. I firmly believe that meetings need not be merely a necessary evil; rather, they can evolve into delightful and effective tools for collaboration when approached correctly. This goes beyond the basics of having a prepared agenda or a checklist of action items. It's about mastering the art of facilitation, nurturing psychological safety, and recognizing that meetings are just one of many collaboration tools at our disposal. Whether you're a facilitator, a meeting host, or an attendee, you have the power to make a difference.

Having worked in Silicon Valley and offices around the world, I've encountered both the highs and lows of corporate life. From attempting to reduce the number of cringeworthy moments we've all faced—such as the time I had to ask for a question to be repeated because I was more focused on my emails than the meeting itself—I've become a passionate advocate for transforming the way teams and organizations convene. The strategies outlined in this book have led to fewer meetings and a measurable increase in engagement and collaboration, whether in person, hybrid, or fully remote. Employing a variety of facilitation techniques, tools, and methods, I've worked to strike a balance between productivity and connectivity.

This book offers collaboration practices and strategies designed to navigate the complexities of today's post-pandemic work life. However, the shift in meeting dynamics goes beyond individual efforts; it necessitates organizational change. One major challenge lies in overcoming resistance from senior executives who are deeply entrenched in traditional meeting cultures. To address this, I provide effective communication strategies tailored to engage senior management and advocate for innovative and flexible collaboration methods. These approaches, ranging from fostering psychological safety to embracing asynchronous communication, aren't mere theoretical concepts; they are practical tools that have proven to significantly boost productivity. The Pro Tips and Exercise sections at the end of each chapter aim to further help you implement these strategies and put them into practice in your own world.

Now let's meet the central characters in this business parable.

Wendy and Bob, middle managers under pressure, find themselves navigating the turbulent waters of post-pandemic work life. They grapple with an unrelenting tide of meetings, often feeling submerged in a flood of requests and vague responsibilities. While their adventures are at times painfully relatable and humorously absurd, they are not mere fiction; they are inspired by my real-life scenarios. Through their experiences, Wendy and Bob uncover groundbreaking collaboration strategies.

Peter, on the other hand, embodies the traits of progressive senior executives I've encountered. He's not just a leader; he's an innovator at heart. He genuinely cares for his team's well-being and eagerly explores new collaboration methods, even if they fail.

Together, Wendy, Bob, and Peter transcend functioning as characters in a mere story for your entertainment. They represent the vanguard of a movement happening today. Their journey provides vital insights and practical methods crucial for organizations adapting to the realities of virtual and hybrid workplaces. Their story unlocks an organization's potential to thrive when it champions meaningful collaboration over meeting attendance.

Get ready to embark on a journey grounded in reality yet geared toward revolutionizing your approach to meetings and work. Allow Wendy, Bob, and Peter to shed light on the true essence of collaboration and productivity in today's ever-evolving work landscape. Fasten your seat belt and prepare for a transformative adventure ahead.

1.
WENDY VS.
THE MEETING MONSTER

DING!

My phone buzzed with a new email, breaking the silence of my all-too-rare moments of focused work. The digital chime pierced the air, sharp and relentless, like a call that demanded attention whether welcome or not. I was about to ignore it but read the notification. It was from Bob, my ever-affable co-worker. *Hi Wendy, could we meet to discuss something with Peter? He wants to have a chat with us.* Peter was our enthusiastic but overly meeting-happy boss and head of our department. Bob had attached a calendar invite that looked like a color-coded painting. I sighed, a sound that had become all too familiar in the midst of this relentless meeting storm.

Odd. Bob usually just messaged me on Slack, our company's messaging app, the lifeline for quick communication. Then I noticed Peter was copied on the email. *Of course. Peter loves meetings.* Whether it was to share news, discuss something, or make a decision, his answer was always the same—book a meeting!

This was so annoying. We didn't need to have a meeting for everything. There were better ways to communicate than booking time on people's calendars and dragging them into video calls.

I shot Bob a Slack message. "Hey, what's this meeting about? Can we chat asynchronously instead, where it is OK to have a delay in our response instead of engaging with each other in real time?" I really didn't want to block any more time on my already-full calendar with another meeting. All these meetings were going to break my concentration, and I needed dedicated time to do the mountain of work on my plate. If we could do this asynchronously, I could then choose to accept any incoming requests (like replying to Bob now) or ignore them until I finished my work or I took a breather. That would allow me to have more time for doing my work.

Bob replied quickly. "Oh, Peter got some news he wants to share with you too. That's why he set up the meeting."

I frowned. Bob and I both knew we didn't need a meeting just to share information. *Why didn't he suggest an alternative to Peter?* Granted, Peter was the executive VP, much more senior than both of us, but I'd never been afraid to speak up, even to senior management.

Taking a deep breath, I replied to the email thread, addressing both Bob and Peter. "Hi Peter, I heard you have some news to share with us. Could we handle this asynchronously? You could send us the information, and we'll provide feedback within an agreed time frame. It might help us eliminate at least one meeting. What do you think?"

Peter replied, "Because we could all do with one less meeting, Wendy, I'll give it a try. But what about sharing news with the whole team? Still no meeting?"

A small thrill of victory surged through me. "I'll set up a private Slack channel for you and the team," I offered. "You can share news whenever you like. Just promise me you won't spam us. ;)"

One meeting request diverted! And we potentially eliminated a big team meeting as well! Whew! That fired up my resolve to cut as many meetings as possible.

Of course, Peter wasn't always that agreeable. But since he seemed open to having fewer meetings, I kept my eyes peeled for any opportunity to capitalize on this preference.

A few weeks later, Peter was grumbling about low productivity, so I volunteered to give him some suggestions. My plan was to point out the glaring problem of meeting-filled days. I scheduled a one-on-one with him to present my case.

To prepare, I created a detailed report highlighting the cost of the meetings—the number of hours we spent in them, the attendees required, the combined salaries—and the resulting drop in productivity. I also included the general sentiment of our colleagues who were equally fed up with endless meetings. Armed with data and a clear plan, I walked with determination to Peter's office and knocked.

"So, Wendy," Peter said, gesturing for me to sit, "what's your take on improving productivity? And remember, our budget's already stretched thin."

I took a deep breath and launched into my presentation. "Peter, one of the reasons for the low productivity is because our department is drowning in meetings. It is impacting our ability to get actual work done. Look at these numbers."

Peter's brow furrowed as he scanned the graphs and charts on my tablet. "While I've always been aware that meetings can impact productivity, your compelling case has really brought home just how significant that impact can be. My days are just as packed—I could definitely use more time to think and get real work done. So what do you suggest we do?"

I leaned forward, my enthusiasm bubbling over. "First, we implement a policy requiring every meeting request to include a clear agenda and defined purpose. We don't attend those that don't meet these criteria."

Peter's eyes lit up. "I like that! It would free up time right away."

"Yes," I agreed, "and this will reinforce the policy and help us weed out unnecessary meetings. Second, we should encourage more asynchronous communication for information sharing, like we discussed before. And finally, we need to provide training on effective collaboration—meetings are only one way to collaborate."

Peter nodded slowly, considering my words. "It's an interesting approach to boosting productivity. Plus, you're saving money and promising fewer meetings at the same time." He paused, then continued. "Alright, let's implement that policy you proposed and give the asynchronous communication a try. But I'm not convinced we need training sessions for it."

I smiled, accepting the compromise. "Thank you, Peter. I appreciate your willingness to try these changes."

As Peter stood, signaling the end of our meeting, he added, "Keep me updated, Wendy. I'm counting on you to make this work."

Leaving his office, I felt a heady mix of relief and satisfaction. I hadn't secured everything I'd hoped for, but it was a good start. With this victory under my belt, I, Wendy the Meeting Slayer, was now on a mission to see what other meetings we could cut from our calendars.

The next chapter of my mission to slay the meeting monster began the very next day as I logged into our team's weekly marathon video meeting. Bob and the rest of the team were already there, their expressions a mix of resignation and boredom as we braced ourselves for Peter's monotonous status updates.

As Peter's voice droned on, my mind began to wander. I had to give him credit—he'd followed my recommendation by including a clear agenda and purpose in the meeting request. But did we really need this meeting every week? Most of us just sat in silence, probably checking emails or daydreaming about anything other than Peter's soporific voice. It felt like such a waste of time.

An idea started forming, and I couldn't wait to share it with Bob. What if we suggested canceling this weekly meeting and replacing it with quick, asynchronous status updates? We could create a system where everyone could easily see if anything needed discussion. If everything went well, then nothing needed to be discussed, and we wouldn't need to have a meeting at all.

As soon as the meeting ended, I messaged Bob. "Hey, now that we got rid of that useless meeting with Peter, what do you think about getting rid of this weekly status meeting too?"

Bob replied almost immediately. "I'm all ears!"

I outlined my idea, explaining how we could set up a simple format on our internal company forum, Wiki, for people to input their status whenever there was an update. "At the end of each work week, everyone can post a traffic light status using written words: red, yellow, green on Slack. We can see at a glance which projects need attention (red or yellow). For anything that needs discussion or has issues, we'd find more details on the Wiki. Otherwise, no need to go to Wiki at all."

Bob's digital avatar nodded in agreement. "Sounds like a good experiment to try. We should give it a month before asking team members what they think. Let them get used to the change first."

As usual, Bob volunteered me to pitch the idea to Peter. I didn't mind; I was ready to champion this change and knew how to approach it with our meeting-loving boss. I suggested that Peter shorten his weekly staff meeting by removing the status portion and focusing only on things that needed discussion. We could read the rest on Slack. To my surprise, Peter agreed it was worth trying.

It was impossible not to feel a sense of accomplishment. Our suggestions were already saving hours of wasted time each week. The meetings we did have were becoming more focused and engaging, and we had only just begun. My mind raced with possibilities—finding more ways to help our team collaborate better, identifying what truly needed a meeting and what didn't, exploring how we could handle things asynchronously, and discovering new methods to work more effectively with our teammates.

Watch out, old boring meetings—I'm coming for you! >:)

PRO TIPS

- Don't expect an immediate response when you are working asynchronously. Instead, be pleasantly surprised when people respond quickly. That's because it is people's choice to respond immediately or wait until they finish what they are doing or when they take a breather (just like Wendy). That's why working asynchronously allows people more time to work uninterrupted.

- A good practice is to explicitly define SLAs (service level agreements) for all requests, including project requests and all communication tools. SLAs are agreements between parties that define the expected level of service, including specific metrics for performance, quality, and responsibilities. They help manage expectations and ensure accountability between parties. These SLAs should be codified so that everyone understands what is expected of them when they get such requests and when to expect responses, thus allowing them to allocate their time accordingly. Here are a couple of examples:

  - An acknowledgement of receipt of email within twenty-four hours and a reply within forty-eight hours.

- An acknowledgement of receipt of Slack message by end of day (or even immediate, if you so desire).

- If you don't have explicit SLAs (or you want to override existing SLAs), you could proactively put an expectation in the actual message, something like "I need an answer in three days."

- As you can see from the story, people, even progressive executives like Peter, are not always agreeable, trusting, or eager to learn. If you want to get executives' buy-in, consider reading my short article "How to Make a Case to Senior Management."[1] Wendy successfully applied many of the strategies discussed in the article, including developing a reputation for responsibility and understanding the executives' goals, interests, and challenges. You might find these strategies helpful too.

EXERCISE

1. Do you call a meeting for everything? Does your boss or your company?

2. Let's reimagine how we work and reevaluate what truly needs a meeting. Write down all the meetings that you have, including recurring meetings and one-off meetings. Then look through the list and see if some of the meetings can be done asynchronously.

3. Now let's go one step further. Look back through the list of meetings that you have and look through what you thought can't be done asynchronously. Are there parts of the meeting that can be done asynchronously? If you don't know, read on and find out.

2.

THE ASYNC ATTACK

A GENTLE BREEZE RUSTLED through the leaves outside my window as I sipped my tea, lost in thought. Weeks had slipped by since Bob and I had embarked on our noble quest to free our calendars from the grip of ineffective meetings. We had made some progress, eliminating some meetings and shortening others, but our calendars were still too packed. Suddenly, an idea flashed through my mind like a bolt of lightning.

With a burst of excitement, I opened Slack and began typing. "Hi Bob! We've done well cutting out those status updates and informational meetings. But what if we took it a step further? What if we taught people that they don't need a meeting just to share or gather information? We could show them how to use Slack or video messages to distribute and collect information asynchronously. We can even link to more in-depth information on our Wiki."

It didn't take long for Bob to respond. "Good thinking, Wendy. I'm not sure everyone knows how to work asynchronously just yet. And speaking of which, didn't Peter want input on the three fun activities he's proposing for the company picnic? Seems like a perfect opportunity to put your theory into practice."

A smile spread across my face as I typed back. "He did! And we need a decision by next week. What if we set up a Slack poll with Peter's options to see which one gets the most votes and an Other category for new ideas?"

I elaborated on the plan, suggesting we keep the poll open for three days to allow for voting and decision-making without a meeting.

"Hmm. What if we get some crazy expensive Other ideas that win?"

I pondered his concern before replying. "Good point. We could state the budget up front and ask people to research costs before proposing new ideas. It'll be a learning opportunity for everyone."

"What if we get a tie?" Bob pressed.

"Then we can either do a tiebreaker poll or, if necessary, call a short meeting to discuss and decide," I responded.

After hashing out a few more details, we felt reasonably confident in our Slack polling plan. I quickly messaged Peter, explaining what Bob and I hoped to do.

Peter's response, however, carried a hint of skepticism. "What if we don't get enough responses in three days?"

Determined to win Peter over, I delved into a more detailed explanation. "I don't expect everyone to vote, but I think we should have enough. If we don't after a day or two, I'll remind people. If we still don't have enough votes, I can: 1) Put a placeholder meeting on everyone's calendars a week from now. Tell people that if we don't get enough votes on Slack, they will have to show up to the meeting. 2) Tell people that this is their time to voice their opinions. If they don't vote, they give up that right, and we'll choose from the votes that we have."

"I like the first option. I think people would be motivated to voice their opinions if it meant avoiding another meeting," Peter replied.

In the end, the Slack voting worked beautifully. Our team got the input we needed, and I eliminated yet another meeting from my calendar. Bob and I exchanged a quick virtual high five, satisfied with our progress. This small but important step toward my goal of a meeting-free future had me brimming with enthusiasm. Suddenly, a familiar sound broke through my reverie: *sssss-crape, knock-knock-knock*—the unmistakable Slack notification. My eyes widened as I saw the sender's name: Peter.

A Slack message from Peter? This is new! He had never originated a one-on-one message from Slack before. I felt a mix of surprise and excitement. For weeks, I'd been gently nudging Peter away from his reliance on excessive meetings and emails, encouraging him to embrace Slack for more efficient communication. This unexpected message was progress.

Peter's inquiry was direct. "Hey Wendy, I noticed you've been rethinking how we do things lately. Are you on some kind of mission to eliminate meetings?"

I couldn't help but grin as I typed my response. "Hey Peter, nice to see you're using Slack more and email less. ;-) And yes, I'm trying to cut back on unnecessary meetings. We talked about this before, remember? My calendar is jammed with back-to-back meetings all day. I can only get real work done after hours these days."

Peter quickly replied. "Yes, I'm getting used to not emailing as much. And you're right, we did discuss it before. Wow, I had no idea your calendar was that overbooked! Is it that bad for others too?"

"Unfortunately yes," I replied. "The back-to-back meetings are so tiring. We really need to change people's minds and habits around scheduling a meeting for every discussion or conversation."

"I agree," Peter wrote. "I've had to block my own calendar just to get work done. Maybe it's time we took a hard look at whether all these meetings are truly necessary."

I nodded unconsciously and began to type. "I think we need to consider the purpose and what we are trying to achieve with these meetings. Then we can figure out if a meeting is the best way to accomplish that goal."

Peter's three gray dots blinked for some time before I saw his response. "You're right, we've been having these weekly meetings out of habit without really evaluating if they are the most effective use of our time."

"Exactly," I continued. "For example, when you had that important news to share last week, instead of calling a special meeting, you simply posted it on Slack. And when we needed to gather input on ideas for the upcoming company picnic, we used Slack polling and got great feedback without a meeting."

"I was surprised by how well the Slack voting worked," Peter admitted. "So are you saying we should scrutinize every meeting invitation and decide if we truly need to meet?"

"Yes, we should always consider the purpose and desired outcome. Did you know there are actually four different types of meetings? Understanding them can help us determine if a meeting is truly the best forum."

"Four types?"

I seized the opportunity to educate him. "Yes, four main

types: to share information, make decisions, collaborate on a problem, or brainstorm ideas."

I reminded Peter of our recent successes, highlighting how we'd already proven that information gathering and sharing and even some decision-making could be handled without meetings. The company picnic fun activity poll was a perfect example.

"Right. But what about the other types you mentioned?"

Encouraged by his interest, I launched into an explanation of how we could handle collaborative problem-solving and brainstorming differently. I gave an example of how I prepared ideas separately before meeting with Bob to finish brainstorming together.

"So you did some of the brainstorming on your own first?" Peter asked.

"That's right," I said. "Because we worked independently on ideas beforehand, our face-to-face time focused on sharing and riffing on each other's ideas to create something even better."

"So you split it into 'my work' and 'our work' essentially," he wrote. His reply showed me that he started to see the logic behind this approach.

"Now you're getting it!" I exclaimed. "The shortened meeting actually focuses on the work we need to do together, not the part we do individually. It forces us to be more prepared, saving time in the long run."

Peter's response was unexpectedly enthusiastic. "That's nice! But how do we ensure people adopt this pattern? I wouldn't have thought of that because it's not what I'm used to doing."

I shared my plans with Peter. "It's definitely a change in thinking. People will need time to adjust. We also need to learn remote facilitation skills."

"Remote facilitation? What's that?" he asked.

I paused, realizing we'd gotten a bit ahead of ourselves. "Hold that thought," I typed. "Let me finish explaining the four meeting types first."

I summarized how we had already replaced meetings for sharing information and making straightforward decisions with asynchronous methods like Slack and voting. "That leaves us with collaborating to solve problems together, which still requires real-time meetings."

"But isn't brainstorming also collaborating in a way?" Peter inquired.

"It is a form of collaboration, yes," I replied, "but by separating independent ideation from synthesizing our thoughts, we minimize the need for constant meetings."

Peter's response showed he'd grasped the core idea. "So we do the individual part first, then come together only if needed."

"Yes," I affirmed. "By the way, I have a cheat sheet that outlines all four types of meetings in bullet points. Let me email it to you."

"Oh, that would be great. Thanks."

Then, to my surprise, he suggested I help teach this new perspective to the rest of the team. My heart leapt with excitement. It wasn't quite the comprehensive training I'd initially proposed, but it was a start.

"Sure!" I eagerly agreed. "I think it'll really help us rethink meetings. By the way, this was part of the training I had initially proposed. :)"

"Really? You mean I should have listened to you from the beginning? ;)" He paused, then he added, "Seriously, I can tell already our team is going to get so much better at this."

I smiled, appreciating his support. "Well, with you as an ally now, I believe it!"

PRO TIPS

- Reminder: In chapter 1, I talked about setting SLAs when working asynchronously. Notice that Wendy is being explicit with the Slack poll. She sets an SLA of three days and uses the threat of forcing a meeting if there's no response.

- When explaining things to executives, even when an agreement is reached, make sure to repeat it multiple times. Just like Peter, executives can be forgetful when they have many other things occupying their minds. Wendy reminded Peter that they had discussed it before, and she went on to detail it again in a different way than when she first presented it to Peter. That is a good way to ensure an executive (or anyone actually) truly understands and remembers a new concept.

- As a review, here are the four main types of meetings:
  - Information sharing
  - Decision-making
  - Problem-solving
  - Brainstorming ideas

EXERCISE

Let's dissect each of the meetings on your list that I asked you to put together in chapter 1.

1. Put the meetings into the four types that Wendy mentioned. We already know that all information sharing can be done asynchronously. You'll end up with fewer meetings.

2. For the meetings that aren't for information sharing, are there parts of the meeting where people can do things on their own in addition to parts that need to be done together? This will tell you where things can be done asynchronously and where you need to meet in real time. This way, the actual meeting time may not be as much as you initially thought. You end up with shorter meetings or fewer meetings.

3.
NAVIGATING THE MEETING MAZE

WITH PETER ON BOARD and a shared goal of transforming our meeting culture, I decided it was time to rope Bob into the mission. After all, he was the one who "voluntold" me to talk to Peter. Payback was in order!

I found Bob in our virtual breakroom, a space in a virtual office app where people, through avatars or live video, can move around and engage in spontaneous conversations, mimicking real-life office interactions. With a sly smile, I cornered him.

"Wendy," Bob said, eyeing me suspiciously. "What's with that mischievous smirk?"

I lowered my voice conspiratorially. "Remember how you 'suggested' I talk to Peter about improving our meetings?"

Bob chuckled. "Ah yes, you were thrilled about that."

I batted my eyelashes playfully. "Well, I did talk to Peter, and you won't believe what he said."

Bob leaned forward, looking eager for the details. "Spill the beans, Wendy."

I recounted my conversation with Peter about the four types of meetings. "Peter gets it, Bob! But he admitted it's not something he's used to, that it's a mindset shift for him."

Bob quickly said, "We need to teach people the thinking behind scheduling a meeting."

"Good idea," I agreed, "and it'll take time for people to adjust. Remember how we used to decline meeting invites without an agenda to get people to think about what they wanted out of the meeting?"

Bob chuckled, recalling our old tactics. "Yeah, we were notorious for that."

"I think we need to start doing something similar again," I suggested. "This time, we should focus on the objective and desired outcome, not just having an agenda. When we receive a meeting invite, we should ask, 'What is the objective? What do you want to achieve?' This will get people thinking about the purpose of the meeting. It trains them to think about the outcome rather than the output and not just having an agenda or collecting action items afterward."

I slumped back in my chair, feeling the weight of my back-to-back meetings. "I can't even do my actual work until the day is over. It's exhausting!"

Bob sympathized. "Yeah, that tactic was effective before, but some people write useless objectives like 'sync up,' which doesn't justify a meeting."

I sighed, frustration creeping into my voice. "A sync-up is mostly information sharing and gathering, which can be done asynchronously on a messaging platform like Slack. We've already shown that's more efficient. Plus it creates a written record we can refer to later, keeping everyone aligned. So even when a meeting invitation states an objective, we should challenge whether a real-time meeting is needed by asking if it can be done asynchronously."

Bob's eyes narrowed in concentration. "Good point. I've had to revisit those records myself more than once. What if we put together some working agreements with teams on when live, synchronous meetings are truly needed versus when asynchronous communication could work instead? We've already started pushing back on informational meetings that could just be an email or Slack thread."

"Before we do that, we need to address another critical issue. People don't know how to facilitate meetings effectively, whether in-person or virtual. We need to teach proper remote facilitation. Otherwise, nothing will change and our calendars will stay packed. Plus, it'll help explain the concept to Peter."

Bob nodded, acknowledging the importance of the skill, but offered a word of caution. "If we try to overhaul everything at once, it'll be too much change too fast. Let's keep it simple and focus on one area at a time."

"You're right," I conceded, recognizing the wisdom in his words. "Baby steps are better. Once someone has defined a meeting objective, they can then decide if parts or all of it could be handled asynchronously. We can model how to outline expectations and deadlines for any pre-meeting work to reduce synchronous time, like we did for the company picnic activity planning. People need to understand that remote facilitation isn't just in-person facilitation with added project management or hounding people to complete tasks."

Bob liked the idea of leading by example. "Why don't we run a facilitation training where the pre-work is contributing questions and ideas asynchronously before the session? That way, we're already teaching some of the asynchronous facilitation techniques that we want teams to adopt. At the same time, we can teach people the new perspective to meetings as Peter wants."

"Brilliant!" I exclaimed. "We can set up a shared document and have them add their thoughts ahead of time to make the session more relevant and impactful. That will demonstrate the techniques we're encouraging."

As we delved deeper into the intricacies of effective meeting preparation and facilitation, Bob, ever the pragmatist, proposed that we put together some guidance on this.

"Sure! Where should we start?"

He paused for a moment, contemplating the best approach. "I think we should create a document with tips and strategies that we could share with others. People need a practical guide to improve their meeting game."

I eagerly agreed. "Absolutely. As someone who has sat through far too many pointless meetings, I'm excited to provide advice on how leaders can make the process more meaningful."

"Well"—Bob began to smile—"I think we should do exactly what we'll be advising others to do. Facilitation starts *way* before any meetings. So let's start by jotting down what we do to prepare for a meeting."

"Great!" I replied, my excitement growing. "I always practice what I preach when it comes to meeting facilitation."

Bob's voice took on a thoughtful cadence as he outlined his process. "I first go through the thinking process we've already taught: to figure out whether I need a meeting or not and whether it should be synchronous or asynchronous. If a meeting is needed, here are six things I consider."

I leaned in, ready to absorb his wisdom.

"First, I think about who I need in that meeting to achieve the goal and outcome while ensuring we have enough viewpoints so we don't miss any angles."

"That's crucial," I said. "We don't want to miss out on valuable perspectives."

Bob nodded. "Next, I consider how to invite the people I've identified. Then, third, what words do I use and what tone do I take?"

"Communication is key. The way you invite people can set the tone for the entire meeting," I chimed in.

"Exactly. Fourth, is there any pre-work for the attendees, and how should that be framed? Fifth, how do I shape the expectations of the meeting? Sixth, what additional communications are needed besides the meeting invite and agenda?"

"I like how you think," I remarked. "We really need to emphasize that an agenda alone isn't enough. People have to be more intentional than just writing, 'Sync to talk about blah-blah-blah.'"

"Yes," Bob agreed. "Let's dive into the six points I mentioned, starting with who we need in the meeting. By the way, I'll email you those six points later. So, the people that we need in any meeting, whether synchronous or asynchronous, include those who have specific information or knowledge about the topic, those who are directly impacted by the decisions made in the meeting, and those who have the authority to make such decisions. Anyone else can read or hear about the decisions later without wasting their time sitting in the meeting. That way, we ensure that we don't have extra people, making the meeting bigger than necessary while either wasting their time or having them slow down the discussion or decision-making process."

"Absolutely! I've noticed that people tend to invite everyone they can think of, just to cover all their bases, afraid someone might feel left out. It's like they're caught up in the FOMO frenzy." I threw my hands up in exasperation. "The problem is, you end up inviting people who aren't necessarily vested in the outcome, and it wastes everyone's time. Some people only need to be informed; they don't need to be in a meeting, as we've discussed before. Do you know how many times I've sat in meetings, trusting others to make the decision without me, where an email summary would've sufficed?"

Bob's expression mirrored my frustration. "It's a common problem. And you've hit on a key issue: trust. When trust is low, everything slows down. We become mired in endless unnecessary meetings, stifled by the fear of delegation. Meetings turn into these massive gatherings with too many voices, all trying to reach consensus. Progress and innovation stall as we get caught in an endless cycle of seeking agreement from everyone. These oversized meetings are just a symptom of that deeper issue. That's why we need to spread the word about this."

Our conversation shifted to discuss a *Forbes* article I had read, titled "Five Reasons Employees Hate Meetings and How Leaders Can Improve the Process."[2] It offers tips for enhancing meetings, such as having an agenda and capturing action items, and the importance of decent facilitation skills to keep the meeting on track and prevent it from spiraling into tangents.

Bob remarked that while those were good steps, they were still somewhat behind the curve in terms of what truly effective meetings entailed. I couldn't agree more.

As our discussion continued, I became increasingly impressed with Bob's well-structured thoughts, especially his six-point framework for effective meeting preparation. "I really like how you've structured it, Bob," I said with genuine appreciation in my voice.

Bob's eyes lit up with satisfaction as he smiled. "Thanks, Wendy. If we can help others navigate this meeting maze more effectively, we'll be making a significant difference in their work lives."

As our conversation drew to a close, I felt a renewed sense of purpose. Our mission to liberate our calendars had evolved into something much bigger—a complete reimagining of how we collaborate and communicate.

PRO TIPS

- After doing the exercises in previous chapters, you should have fewer and/or shorter meetings. Now you have the time to properly design and prepare for the truly necessary synchronous meetings.

- Once a synchronous meeting is deemed necessary, even with asynchronous parts, go through Bob's six-point framework for effective meeting preparation:

    1. Who do I need in that meeting to achieve the goal and outcome while having enough viewpoints so we don't miss any angles?

    2. How do I invite the people I've identified?

    3. What words do I use, and what tone do I take?

    4. Is there any pre-work for the attendees, and how do I frame that work?

    5. How do I shape the expectations of the meeting?

    6. What pieces of communication are needed on top of the meeting invitation with an agenda?

EXERCISE

You've already identified whether a live, synchronous meeting is necessary (refer to the four types of meetings described in chapter 2) and if there are parts that can be asynchronous (this depends on the objective of the meeting). Now examine the invitees of the live, synchronous meetings. Are they all necessary? Ask these questions to decide:

1. Do your meeting attendees pay full attention throughout the meeting or do they check their phones and work on their laptops most of the time?

2. If you have a question for them, do you have to repeat the question when you call their names?

These are signs that those people are not needed in that meeting, or at least not the entire meeting. It may be time to rethink how you structure your meeting.

4.
INVITING INTENTIONALLY

BOB AND I SPENT THE NEXT FEW DAYS IMMERSED in our collaborative effort, working diligently on the material for the upcoming company training on running effective meetings. We delved into the intricacies of meeting preparation and facilitation.

One afternoon, while we were in our company's virtual office, I decided to steer our conversation toward the second point in Bob's framework: extending invitations to attendees. I wanted to ensure we left no stone unturned. Leaning forward with curiosity, I said, "Bob, let's talk about how to actually extend the invitation. Your point number two, remember? I assume you don't mean we just send a meeting invitation, right?"

Bob, ever the strategic thinker, leaned back in his chair and offered a small smile. "Your assumption is correct, Wendy," he replied, his voice steady and measured. "The key element many organizers overlook is being intentional. As the meeting creator, you need to carefully consider both what you need from each attendee to achieve the desired outcome and, even more importantly, what's in it for them. Most people think about the former but not the latter. The best way to structure the invitation is by explicitly explaining why it is useful for them and their team. They want the meeting to move things forward as much as you do. Remember, it's not about you, it's about them. Taking time to think through their motivations can help you narrow down and refine the invite list too. If you can't articulate a clear benefit for someone, they most likely don't need to be there. They might only need to be informed."

As Bob explained, I began to grasp the importance of crafting the invitation step by step with precision. First, it should clearly state the main purpose or goal for the meeting. People want to know why their time is worth spending. Second, it should spell out what makes each invitee uniquely qualified to weigh in, demonstrating that their particular expertise or point of view is valued. Lastly, it should explain what's in it for them—how attending directly benefits them or their team. When meeting makers clearly outline the objective, tap into the team's self-interest, and show they want the team's input, people are more likely to attend and engage. No more generic "sync up" objectives!

My racing mind screeched to a halt as a new thought struck me. "Wait a second," I said, tilting my head slightly as I processed this new idea. "When you say we should spell out what makes each invitee uniquely qualified, are you suggesting we send a fully customized invitation to every single person?" My eyes widened at the prospect, imagining late nights hunched over my computer, crafting dozens of individualized messages.

Bob's usually calm demeanor cracked for a moment as he realized my misunderstanding. "Oh, goodness no!" he exclaimed, waving his hands emphatically. "Just one invitation for everyone. The magic lies in crafting the wording in a way that resonates with each person. They should read it and instantly think, 'That's why I'm needed, and here's how I can contribute.' It's about creating a collective sense of purpose without the need for custom invitations."

I let out an exaggerated sigh of relief, dramatically wiping imaginary sweat from my brow. "Whew! You had me worried there for a minute, Bob!" I said with a chuckle. "I thought I'd be up all night writing individualized invitations to each person."

Bob's eyes crinkled with amusement as he chuckled softly. "Don't worry. One thoughtful invite will do the trick!"

As the laughter subsided, I found myself tapping my chin, lost in thought. "So, it's an art, isn't it?" I mused. "Structuring the invitation in the way that feels personalized to each recipient without the painstaking task of customizing each invitation?"

Bob nodded with an encouraging smile. "Indeed," he replied, his calm voice a stark contrast to my bubbling excitement. "The art lies in the precise steps outlined earlier, which allow you to craft more meaningful messages, the words chosen, and the tone adopted. It's about conveying mutual benefits, making people attend because they genuinely want to, not out of obligation or guilt. Nor is it a status symbol to be invited."

"That's fascinating!" I smiled, the lightbulb going off in my mind. "Crafting invitations that not only communicate but resonate, creating genuine interest. So collaboration becomes more than just a meeting; it becomes a shared journey where individuals willingly participate, understanding the tangible benefits for themselves."

Bob, delighted with my comprehension, snapped his fingers and pointed at me with a mischievous smile. "Exactly! Collaboration thrives when individuals genuinely want to participate because they recognize the value for themselves. It's an art and a science, Wendy!"

Our conversation shifted when Bob brought up the topic of pre-work. I jumped in with curiosity. "If there are assignments for attendees to complete before the meeting, how should I frame and communicate those?"

Bob leaned forward, his face clear on my screen. "Any pre-work is intended to make the synchronous meeting itself more effective and focused. It can be for you as the organizer or for the different participants. Given people's busy schedules, you never want to overload them with meeting pre-work."

He cautioned against using a demanding tone that guilt-trips people into completing the tasks. Instead, he suggested clearly explaining how finishing the pre-work would enable them to contribute better and get more value from the synchronous discussion. Providing guidelines for how long the pre-work should take, like setting aside fifteen minutes, helps attendees understand and manage expectations. Sending the invitation with enough lead time, ideally at least a week in advance, for them to prepare is also crucial.

Unable to resist injecting a bit of humor, I quipped, "But if we don't guilt people into the pre-work, no one will do it!"

Bob joined in with a hearty laugh, his face filling the screen. "Again, it goes back to tone and intentional wording. If the invitation successfully communicates the benefits and relevance of the pre-work for achieving those benefits, people will naturally see how it helps them and their goals. Go beyond vague instructions and offer guidance like 'set aside fifteen minutes to do the pre-work' or 'if you're doing this longer than fifteen minutes, you're overthinking or overdoing this.'"

"Ah, so basically you're setting up the right expectations of what the pre-work entails so that they can better prepare themselves."

Bob nodded in agreement. "More importantly, we want the pre-work to be impactful but lightweight. We don't want them to feel that they have tons more work to do—before we even have a meeting."

Just as I was about to burst with another question, a chat notification from our boss, Peter, popped up on my screen. I couldn't help mentioning it to Bob. "Peter has been using Slack a lot more often than email lately. I think we are really rubbing off on him!"

Bob grinned. "We are definitely influencing positive change in Peter bit by bit!"

"Speaking of change, to summarize our discussion," I said, "We have discussed your thought process on how to evaluate whether we really need to drag everyone into a live meeting or if we can just get away with pinging each other asynchronously. You know, avoiding the whole 'meeting for the sake of a meeting' debacle."

"Exactly, Wendy," Bob responded. "And if you decide that a synchronous meeting is a must, remember the golden rules."

I nodded to myself, ticking off points on my fingers. "It's about inviting the smallest group that can still offer diverse viewpoints. Crafting the invitation with intentional wording and tone, focusing on articulating what's in it for them, not making them think they're being summoned nor attaching a status symbol to being invited. Framing any pre-work in a similar mutually beneficial way. And, of course, making sure to set clear expectations around the objective, agenda, and next steps so that everyone knows what's expected of them—like a well-orchestrated play."

Bob's response came swiftly, his voice tinged with amusement. "Yes, and make sure the pre-work doesn't feel like homework. It should feel more like . . . preparation for a grand adventure."

I laughed. "Oh, Bob! You always make even the most mundane tasks sound epic! I love it!" Still chuckling, I added, "So that covers your points one through five. But what about point number six? Any other communication tricks up your sleeve to ensure our meeting isn't a total snooze fest?"

Bob's reply was almost immediate, as if he'd been anticipating the question. "Send a reminder two days before the meeting—a gentle nudge about the pre-work and a reiteration of how vital their contributions are. It's like setting the stage for a great performance."

"Are two days before the meeting enough time?" I asked.

"Let's experiment!" Bob suggested. We agreed to ask for feedback on what lead time worked best for people.

With that, I felt a sense of accomplishment. Bob and I had covered all the key bases in terms of thoughtfully preparing for and inviting people to a productive meeting. Bob concurred, so we called it a wrap, ready to put our knowledge into practice, determined to free ourselves and our colleagues from endless unproductive meetings, one step at a time.

PRO TIPS

- Make sure you have an outcome in mind for every meeting. Outcomes are not outputs. The outcome is the purpose or the goal of the meeting, which is always having a clearer direction to go toward.

- Some outputs come in the form of decisions made, ideas to pursue, things to research or tasks to complete. If these outputs allow you to know which direction to go, then you've achieved the outcome of the meeting (i.e., you now have a clearer picture of what path to take).

- Information sharing doesn't tell people which direction to go, so it does not warrant a meeting. Most information gathering doesn't warrant a meeting with multiple attendees. It can be done asynchronously; it can be done in the form of an interview. The information gathered can lead to a potential meeting: the information may feed into a brainstorming session or a collaborative work session or a decision to be made.

EXERCISE

1. Now that you know who to invite to your live, synchronous meetings (from the exercise in chapter 3), use the suggestions that Bob and Wendy discussed in this chapter to craft at least one invitation.

2. Once you've finished crafting your invitation, go back to the list of invitees. For each person, ask yourself, "Would they resonate with the invitation? Why or why not?" If you are not sure, it's a good idea to reword the invitation.

3. If you find after a few rewrites that the invitation still may not resonate with a particular person, then ask yourself if that person is really needed for this meeting.

5.
THE FACILITATION
FORMULA

I COULD BARELY CONTAIN MY EXCITEMENT as Bob and I delved into meeting facilitation. "I've been eagerly looking forward to this part of our training prep!" My words tumbled out in a rush.

Bob chuckled. "I can see that, Wendy. Now that we're discussing what happens during a meeting, we need to consider not just the agenda but the whole dynamic and flow. We should model these techniques ourselves during the training sessions too."

"Excellent point," I said, trying to rein in my excitement. "But remote facilitation is so much more than that!"

"You're right," Bob said with a slight smile. "Let's start with basic facilitation skills that work for both in-person and remote settings, then we'll highlight the differences. Any good meeting needs a beginning, middle, and end, like a movie plotline. We need to be intentional and clear in each section."

His insights were always on point, and I admired his ability to distill complex ideas into actionable steps. Inspired, I started bouncing ideas off him. "Oooh, what if we give people five minutes at the start to review asynchronous contributions and get in the right mindset? I hate doing nothing while waiting for people to arrive."

"Love it! It's a smart way to get people aligned up front. Plus, latecomers shouldn't disrupt those who showed up prepared and on time. Let's incorporate this into our training to establish new meeting norms."

Another thought popped into my mind. "Oh! We should set a hard rule that if even one person is remote, everyone joins individually on their own devices whether you're in the meeting room with others or by yourself in your own location. No room cameras projecting groups sitting together! Remote participants deserve equal footing."

"100 percent agree," Bob said. "As facilitators and trainers, we have the responsibility to ensure every attendee can participate fully, whether their camera is on or off."

"Right," I pressed on. "We should highlight the VARK model—Visual, Aural, Read/Write, and Kinesthetic modes of engagement.[3] It's important to use multiple modes since everyone processes information differently. We don't want some people to dominate and others to disengage."

"Too often, facilitators assume their preferred mode is the only way," Bob said with frustration. "How many times have you heard 'It would be good to turn on your video, but if you can't, that's fine'? That disclaimer doesn't make the request okay. They've already announced their preference, making others feel they need to comply. That's not a good way to motivate people to engage."

"Exactly! Facilitators need to get out of their comfort zone and learn new skills. It's not about them; it's about the meeting's outcome and the participants. We shouldn't even mention cameras at all; that creates an unnecessary issue. If the meeting uses multiple modes, people will participate and engage."

Bob's expression softened. "You're right, Wendy. Meeting hosts need to be skilled facilitators, not just old-school agenda managers who collect a list of action items at the end. Facilitators should take time to design the full flow of the entire meeting, like a movie, to ensure the meeting outcome is achieved with maximum engagement, participation, and input from all participants."

Our vision for revolutionizing meetings was crystallizing. "So we've covered setting the stage at the start by aligning to asynchronous pre-work. Now, let's dive into the actual meeting itself. Since there are different types of meetings, we should be specific. For brainstorms, what about starting with a quick check-in to gauge everyone's state of mind? Something lightweight so we have time to hear from everyone."

Bob tilted his head. "Tell me more," he prompted gently.

"We can ask people to give a one-word adjective—*excited, tired, frustrated, puzzled*—to describe their mood, where they're at, or their reactions to the async work," I explained.

Understanding dawned on Bob's face. "I see. So after using the first five minutes to align everyone with the asynchronous work, we take a quick pulse. That way, we facilitators can read the room—gauge the mood and energy levels, identify any concerns or distractions, and adjust our approach as needed."

"Precisely! It also fosters a sense of inclusion and participation right from the start, making everyone feel heard and valued."

Bob's eyes lit up. "I like it. Any ideas on how to do this efficiently?"

I pondered for a moment. "If we're all in the same room, we can simply go around and ask for the one-word adjective. If at least one person is virtual, we could use a 'chatterfall' in the video conference chat. Everyone types their word but doesn't hit send until we give the signal."

"Fabulous!" Bob exclaimed. "And for decision-making meetings, after that initial alignment, I'd ask which portion people disagree with or need more info on. Those become our focus areas for discussion, driving us toward closure and a decision by the end of the meeting."

Our ideas began to flow seamlessly. "For our own training, since we didn't ask for pre-work, we'll use the first ten minutes to ask what people's expectations are. We can give them a (virtual) whiteboard with sticky notes, have them write in silence for five minutes, then share their sticky notes and spend another five minutes reading others'. What do you think?"

"Love it," Bob confirmed. "I think that covers it all."

The excitement in our conversation was palpable. "Now that we've covered the first five to ten minutes, the rest of the meeting follows the agenda. But there's an art to that—it's not just calling out each item. Again, it's back to the facilitation skills. The host or facilitator needs to guide people through the items interactively and engagingly."

Bob's eyes sparkled. "Interactive and engaging techniques for sure! Like Liberating Structures! They're so much fun! They get everyone involved, whether they're introverts or extroverts, talkative or quiet. Liberating Structures can transition the different pieces seamlessly. You can even string several structures together to create a highly interactive meeting that generates diverse insights and options."

I cocked my head quizzically. "Liberating Structures? What are those?"

"Oh!" Bob's eyes widened. "I forgot you're not familiar with them, Wendy. You're missing out! Liberating Structures are tools and facilitation techniques that encourage broader participation and draw out diverse perspectives. Everyone, whether in person or remote, gets a fair shot at participating, experiencing meetings and collaborations in refreshing ways. You can find more information on the website at LiberatingStructures.com."

As he spoke, a memory flickered through my mind, and I interrupted him. "Wait, was that what we used for our virtual Start-of-the-Year party? The one on that fun platform, Kumospace, where people could move around like in real life?"

Bob beamed. "Precisely! Remember how we led the teams through a retrospective of the past year and helped them plan for the coming one? People thought it was just a party with games, but those 'games' were various Liberating Structures."

"No way!" I gasped. "People were stunned to learn it was essentially a work session. They'd been working the entire two hours, but they didn't want it to end!" I chuckled at the memory. "It really shows the power of good facilitation to fully engage people while being productive. It emphasizes the need for meeting hosts to elevate their facilitation skills."

Bob laughed. "Totally! The goal is to make it so lively and enjoyable that time flies by. The perfect antidote to meeting fatigue!"

"Speaking of facilitation skills," he continued, "have you ever been in meetings where people go off on tangents, derailing the agenda?"

I shuddered. "Painfully, yes. Unfortunately, most meeting hosts don't know how to steer the discussion back on track."

"That's why strong facilitation is crucial," Bob said. "A skilled facilitator can guide the dialogue back while keeping everyone focused. If the conversation really veers off, they'll step in firmly but politely to cut it off and direct the group back on course."

"Indeed," I chimed in. "Designating a space to write down off-topic ideas helps too. If they're worth exploring further, suggest revisiting them later. Something like, 'That's interesting. Let's circle back after we cover the current items.' And of course, facilitators need to model that focused behavior and avoid getting sidetracked themselves."

"Absolutely," Bob said with a chuckle. "Once all agenda items are tackled, it's time to wrap up. Reflect on the work, celebrate progress, and translate it into actionable next steps."

"Ooh! A quick summary and alignment check at the end to ensure everyone leaves on the same page."

Bob snapped his fingers. "Yes. Facilitators can quickly gauge agreement by asking for a thumbs-up or -down on the summary. For those who disagree, delve into what doesn't align with their understanding. That allows for quick clarification and resolution before the meeting ends."

"That's brilliant! Though even after the meeting ends, the facilitation isn't over. I don't mean having a project manager nag about action items. But again, it's back to asynchronous work, and we've talked about how to facilitate those."

Bob nodded appreciatively. "Good point. And before the meeting ends, I'd recommend getting some quick feedback. A brief retrospective or a few questions can help assess if we've achieved the outcome, how participants feel about the meeting, and areas for improvement. For decision-making meetings, why not add a quick, fun celebration for reaching a decision?"

I couldn't resist teasing him. "Always up for a party, huh, Bob?"

He grinned unapologetically. "Can't go wrong with celebrating achievements!"

I shifted to a more contemplative tone. "But Bob, can we really expect Peter to facilitate like this? Our boss isn't exactly known for his . . . finesse."

"You have a point. We need to train Peter and the other executives. And"—he paused dramatically—"I officially nominate you, Wendy, to tell Peter what we've been up to."

I gasped in mock horror before bursting into laughter. "Wow, thanks for 'voluntelling' me, Bob!" I shook my head in amusement. "You're too kind!"

PRO TIPS

- Wendy mentioned that there is no need to mention cameras at all in any meetings. However, there is one situation where you may want to, and that is when the meeting is being recorded. For privacy reasons, you may want to specifically tell the attendees that they can turn off their cameras if they do not want to appear in the recording.

- Remember, having an agenda beforehand and capturing action items with owners attached afterward doesn't qualify as a successful meeting. I recommend the following metrics instead:

  - The purpose of the meeting is achieved.

  - Meeting participants feel they have contributed and they're heard.

  - Meeting participants' time is well used.

  - Meeting participants are engaged.

- No one had even realized Wendy and Bob facilitated an entire work session during their Start-of-the-Year party! That is not a fictional party. It actually happened in real life. The attendees' comments in the story are actual feedback from the participants in that party/meeting, demonstrating the concept of "play at work." You can

find out more about the concept at https://www.
playficient.com/play-at-work/ or search for "play
at work" online.

- When designing a meeting, consider using
GenAI tools like Claude or ChatGPT to help
brainstorm the flow. However, think of GenAI
as a diligent mid-level assistant—their input is
valuable, but your facilitation skills are crucial.
You'll need to critically evaluate their suggestions
to ensure they align with your meeting's goals
and participants' needs.

- When you are experimenting or implementing
new ways of working, don't forget about your
boss. Bring them along on your journey. They
can be open to change if you approach them the
same way you would when inviting someone to
your meeting: Figure out the outcome you would
like and also what's in it for them. Watch out for
your tone and the words that you use. Make sure
you mutually agree on the expectations.

EXERCISE

From the previous chapter exercises, you have identified what meetings to have, decided who to invite, and crafted at least one invitation for one meeting. Now it's time to start planning how to run the meeting (i.e., facilitate) so that the meeting will satisfy the metrics that I described in the Pro Tips above. Use what I outlined in this chapter to start building your meeting.

1. First five minutes: Alignment—have people review all the asynchronous contributions to get them in the right mindset.

2. Beginning: Quick one-word check-in

3. Next: Design the agenda in an inclusive and engaging manner for all participants, whether remote or in person. Don't just expect to call out each agenda item. You can make it more engaging by using techniques like Liberating Structures (LS) for each of your agenda items. LS is not time-consuming activities. It can help you efficiently and effectively satisfy all the meeting metrics I described in the Pro Tips above. But don't forget to budget enough time for each item.

4. End: Add the ending that is appropriate for your meeting.

6.
SAFETY DANCE

A FEW DAYS LATER, I was deep in concentration at my desk when the familiar *sssscrape, knock-knock-knock* of an incoming Slack message snapped me out of my focus. Glancing at the upper right corner of my screen, I saw Peter's name pop up with a request for an impromptu video call, which piqued my curiosity, and I quickly hit the call button.

"Hey, Wendy!" Peter's face appeared on my screen, his expression a blend of curiosity and anticipation. "I was just talking with Bob about your new approaches to meetings. It sounds like you two are making some changes in how we think about collaboration and group interactions. Looks like we've got quite a learning curve ahead of us."

I nodded, my tone reassuring. "It's definitely a change, but don't worry. Bob and I are committed to modeling these techniques. With practice, it'll become second nature, like breathing."

Peter's shoulders relaxed a bit. "That's good to hear. I'll need your help to get this right."

"You can count on us," I replied with a playful salute, encouraged by Peter's openness to learning. It was a promising sign for the changes ahead.

Then his expression grew more serious. "While I have you, Wendy . . . Our video production team has been struggling lately—missed deadlines, people transferring to other teams or just quitting. Any thoughts on how we can turn things around?"

I paused, thinking carefully. "Actually, I've observed some of their meetings recently. While there are immediate issues to address, I think there's a deeper problem at play—a lack of psychological safety. From what I saw, many team members don't feel comfortable speaking up or being vulnerable."

Peter's face scrunched up in confusion. "Psycho-what now?"

I chuckled. "Psychological safety. It's about being able to express opinions and ideas without fear of embarrassment or punishment. It's the foundation of productive interactions and strong relationships."

Peter leaned back in his chair, mulling it over. "I see. . . . So why don't they feel safe to speak up? And more importantly, how do we fix it?"

"This isn't something we can tackle in a quick conversation," I cautioned. "It's a complex issue that deserves more time and attention. Rushing it could do more harm than good. How about we set up a dedicated meeting to dive into this? Maybe sometime next week?"

"Sounds good," Peter agreed, looking both relieved and intrigued. "Thanks, Wendy. I know I can always count on you."

As soon as the call ended, I knew I had to loop in my partner in crime. My fingers flew across the keyboard as I fired off a quick Slack message: "Bob! You won't believe the chat I just had with Peter. He's open to improving his meeting facilitation skills and wants our help thinking through meetings more effectively."

Bob's reply was swift. "Sure, happy to help."

"Great, because I may have volunteered you," I wrote, adding a wink emoji, confident in Bob's support. "Oh, and Peter mentioned the video team struggling. He asked how to help them."

"The video team?" Bob's response carried a hint of concern. "What's going on?"

I gave Bob a summary and explained Peter's request. "I sat in on some of their meetings and noticed issues with psychological safety. Peter didn't understand what that meant, so we need to align our approach before discussing it with him."

"Good thinking," Bob replied. "Without proper context, it'll just confuse him more."

"I did explain psychological safety as the belief that you won't be punished or humiliated for speaking up with ideas, questions, concerns, or mistakes."

"That's a good start," Bob said. "What context should we share with Peter? What exactly did you notice in the meetings?"

"Ugh, it was painful! The team lead kept pulling rank. You know, the whole 'I've been doing this forever' and 'I'm the boss' routine. It really stifles open dialogue."

"Yikes! That's certainly problematic," Bob replied. "Perhaps we should compile a list of low psychological safety indicators to compare against your observations. It might help clarify the situation for Peter."

"Good idea," I agreed. "Without psychological safety, people don't ask questions, suggest new ideas, admit mistakes, or think critically. They accept the status quo. I think that just about describes the video production team!"

"Unfortunately, many leaders don't realize that compromising psychological safety leads to disengagement. People adopt various ways to protect themselves. I've seen some individuals choosing to lie low to avoid drawing attention, doing the bare minimum to survive. Others go on the offense and start pointing out others' mistakes. Top performers often look for opportunities elsewhere. This can result in constant turnover."

Recalling past toxic environments, I nodded vigorously, forgetting that Bob couldn't see me. "So true. With psychological safety, people feel comfortable being vulnerable, supporting each other, suggesting ideas, flagging issues, admitting mistakes, and debating constructively. That's how you build high-performing teams."

"Precisely," Bob said. "However, some managers still believe that fear is the only way to establish authority and control, thinking it drives people to work harder."

I shuddered, thinking of past encounters with such leadership styles. "What those managers fail to understand is that management by fear only creates the illusion of control. While it may appear that goals are being met, it ultimately stifles the innovation, creativity, and collaboration needed to navigate our complex and rapidly changing business environment," I explained.

"You're absolutely right."

"BTW, can I call you to continue our chat on psychological safety?" I asked.

"Certainly."

I hit the call button and soon heard Bob's calm voice. "So, what's more to discuss?"

Eager to share, I asked, "Are you familiar with Dr. Amy Edmondson? She's a professor at Harvard Business School who

popularized the term 'psychological safety.' Her research identified four key components for fostering innovation, creativity, and
collaboration in the workplace."

"Four components?" Bob sounded puzzled. "I thought it
was just about feeling safe to share ideas without repercussions."

I chuckled. "There's a bit more to it than that. Would you
like me to elaborate?"

"Please do," Bob replied, his curiosity evident.

I was thrilled by his interest. "First, Inclusion and Diversity,
promoting an environment where everyone feels valued. Second,
Attitude to Risk and Failure, encouraging a mindset that views
mistakes as opportunities to learn. Third, Willingness to Help,
fostering a culture where support is readily available. And finally,
Open Conversation, ensuring everyone is comfortable expressing
their thoughts and opinions."

Bob paused, then said, "That's quite comprehensive. Could
you provide more detail on these components?"

"Of course," I continued. "Dr. Edmondson found that team
members who feel included are more likely to speak up and participate actively. Also, teams that take risks and keep innovating
don't hold mistakes against each other. Blame makes people fear-
ful of failure."

"That makes sense. Can't innovate without taking risks,"
Bob said thoughtfully. "What about the helping aspect?"

"Edmondson discovered that when team members aren't
able to help each other or feel appreciated, teams become unsafe.
Appreciation and support are key," I explained.

"I can see how that fosters goodwill."

"Exactly," I said. "And finally, she found that candor in conversations helps tackle hard problems better. Open, nonjudgmental communication is crucial."

"I see. So psychological safety is not about making sure team members 'feel good.' It's really about creating an environment optimized for engagement, creativity, and performance overall."

"Precisely!" I exclaimed, pleased with Bob's insight. "It truly benefits both the employees and the organization as a whole."

"What about diversity? Does that refer only to demographics?"

"Not at all. While it includes aspects like gender, age, religion, race, and sexual orientation, it also encompasses cognitive diversity and neurodiversity. Simply put, diversity is anything that is different from you. It's these different perspectives and work styles that enrich our teams and enhance our problem-solving capabilities."

"Ah, like our VARK learning styles training. That's a type of diversity too, right?"

"Totally," I confirmed. "But having diversity isn't enough. We need inclusion to make people feel welcomed and valued."

Bob's voice softened. "That reminds me of Vernā Myers' quote: Diversity is being invited to the party. Inclusion is being asked to dance. ™"

"Oh, I love that quote!" I responded appreciatively. "It captures the essence perfectly."

Bob then asked, "So what concrete steps can we take to build psychological safety?"

"One effective method comes from Modern Agile [4]," I replied. "Modern Agile is a community for people interested in uncovering better ways of getting awesome results. One of their guiding principles is to make safety a prerequisite. They suggest establishing meeting safety by agreeing to be CLEAR at the start."

"Agreeing to be clear? Aren't we always clear?"

I chuckled, realizing I needed to explain. "CLEAR is an acronym, Bob. It stands for Curious, caring and open-minded, Listen to one another, Encourage everyone to contribute, Avoid dominating or interrupting, and Repeat and review people's points."

"I see," Bob acknowledged slowly. "So how do we implement this?"

I took a deep breath and launched into my explanation. "Right after we align everyone at the start, we ask, 'Can we agree to be CLEAR?' It's a commitment to keeping an open mind, being curious, and caring about what others have to say during the meeting. It also means really listening to understand first, rather than immediately responding or judging. You know those moments when you start to say something, and someone immediately shuts you down or dismisses you before you can even finish?"

"I hate when that happens," Bob groaned. "It makes me not want to be in the meeting anymore."

"Understandable," I said. "That's a sign of broken psychological safety. Asking people to agree to listen fully first can help avoid those frustrating and unproductive interactions."

"So agreeing to be CLEAR is how we start building psychological safety."

PRO-TIPS

- The directness between Wendy and Peter may seem unusual in some cultures, but it stems from a foundation of trust. This dynamic develops when you've proven yourself reliable, as shown by Peter's statement to Wendy: "I know I can always count on you." Such trust is built when you consistently demonstrate dependability and when your boss recognizes your ability to solve problems effectively, like Wendy's novel idea that helped address part of the low productivity issue that Peter was concerned about. To reach this level of trust, focus on two key aspects:

  1. Develop a reputation for responsibility, as Wendy has done. Being responsible makes you dependable.

  2. Demonstrate a deep understanding of your boss' goals, interests, and challenges so that you can help solve their issues.

Once you've established this foundation, your boss will likely come to trust you as Peter trusts Wendy. This trust leads to more open and direct communication, especially in one-on-one settings.

- You may notice that Wendy "voluntold" Bob in the story. Normally, "voluntelling" someone not only breaks psychological safety, it disempowers people. However, in Wendy and Bob's case, they have worked together for a while, they know each other well, and they have a rapport with each other—a hallmark of a relationship built on psychological safety. Wendy knows that Bob would do the task anyway, so she volunteered herself and Bob to it. You saw in their next conversation that Bob was happy to do that task before knowing Wendy had already volunteered both of them.

- Management by fear, also known as fear-based leadership, is an effective way to demolish psychological safety. It is a psychologically unsafe environment. To gauge if you are in such an environment, ask yourself, Do I or my company do any of the following?

    1. Say things like "If you don't like what's happening, there's the door."

    2. Publicly criticize or embarrass employees (e.g., yell at employees, berate them, or belittle them) in front of others.

3. Constantly monitor and control every aspect of an employee's work and/or implement excessive surveillance measures to monitor employees' every move.

4. Impose harsh and arbitrary punishments for minor mistakes.

5. Withhold important information, creating a culture of secrecy and threats.

6. Openly or covertly engage in bullying or harassing behaviors.

7. Create a competitive and hostile atmosphere, fostering a culture of mistrust.

8. React unpredictably to situations, using anger or punishment without consistency.

9. Show clear favoritism toward certain employees while treating others unfairly.

10. Dismiss or punish or display passive aggressive behavior toward employees who provide constructive feedback or express concerns.

If you answer yes to any of the statements above, then you have a culture of managing by fear.

- Reminder: CLEAR stands for—

  - Curious, caring and open-minded

  - Listen to one another

  - Encourage everyone to contribute

  - Avoid dominating or interrupting

  - Repeat and review people's points

- There's much more to psychological safety than what we cover in this book. If you're interested in exploring examples of teams with low safety, taking a deeper dive into Dr. Amy Edmondson's four components of psychological safety, or accessing additional exercises to enhance psychological safety in your teams, I highly recommend checking out my self-paced Foundation of Psychological Safety online course: https://munwaic. com/online-courses/foundation-of-psychological-safety/ (discount code: Wendy).

EXERCISE

1. Reflect on previous meetings that you've had. Were there any moments when you (or others) felt unsafe? If so, what triggered them?

2. In your next meeting, try CLEAR.

   a. Ask, "Can we agree to be CLEAR?" Then explain what CLEAR stands for.

   or

   b. In the meeting invitation, explain CLEAR as expected agreement on how to behave in the meeting. Then when you start the meeting, ask "Can we agree to be CLEAR?" to confirm agreement and refresh the meaning of CLEAR if needed.

7.
CLEAR
SKIES AHEAD

"SHOULD WE DO THIS CLEAR exercise at the start of every meeting?" Bob continued.

"Generally, yes," I confirmed. "This is an agreement on how people will behave in the meeting. Asking 'Can we agree to be CLEAR?' reminds everyone of the agreed expectations. If someone doesn't act that way, we can call them out during the meeting. That is how to build psychological safety step-by-step."

Bob spoke slowly, so I could tell the pieces were falling into place. "I get it now. By making it a consistent practice, that's how you gradually build psychological safety."

"Exactly!" I replied. "It might feel a bit awkward at first, but with time, it really can work wonders."

"And when you mentioned calling people out, what did you mean by that?" Bob asked.

"As part of the CLEAR agreement," I explained, "anyone on the team, whether it's the CEO or the newest intern, can point out when someone isn't adhering to the agreed-upon behavior. For example, if someone agrees to listen openly but then shuts down an idea, we can gently remind them of the meeting rules we've all committed to. It's a way to course-correct in real time."

Bob snapped his fingers. "Of course! By holding each other accountable, you reinforce the safety while discussions are happening."

"You got it!" I cheered. "Psychological safety gets built step-by-step through those consistent touches. Not overnight but over time, meeting by meeting."

Excitement was evident in Bob's voice as he said, "And that allows teams to eventually tackle really hard issues without fracturing the underlying trust."

"Bingo!" I exclaimed, matching his energy. "When psychological safety is solid, you can have heated but productive debates."

"I'm starting to see how this could be a game changer for our teams. But I'm curious, should we apply these practices only to specific meetings or projects?"

"Great question," I said, appreciating his thoughtful approach. "While we typically start with CLEAR in regular team meetings, its principles extend beyond that—to every interaction, every day. The more consistently we practice CLEAR, the stronger our psychological safety net becomes for the entire team."

"So it's not just about meetings. It's about fostering a culture of psychological safety throughout our entire work environment?"

"That's right!" I confirmed with a broad smile. "Meetings are just one piece of the puzzle. The real impact comes from embedding these principles into all our interactions, from casual breakroom chats to intense brainstorming sessions. When everyone understands and lives by these principles, that's when we see a profound shift in our team dynamics. It's not just about changing meetings; it's about transforming our entire workplace culture!"

Bob paused, then raised another point. "That makes me think about the video team. Besides pulling rank during meetings, does the team lead undermine safety in daily interactions too?"

"Excellent observation, Bob!" I replied, appreciating his perceptiveness. "Unfortunately, yes. That team lead tends to assert authority in everyday interactions as well. It's a significant concern because that behavior steadily erodes the team's psychological safety."

"So the team lead is violating the *A* in CLEAR by dominating and interrupting," Bob said.

"Very good! It's really about respect. A good facilitator should be vigilant about any behavior that could undermine that, be it dominating conversations, interrupting others, or displaying dismissiveness. We have to embody the respectful behavior we want to see."

"You're right. That's what the video team lead does, disrespecting others—pulling rank, interrupting people, dismissing their input. No wonder you said there's a deeper problem of a lack of psychological safety at play."

"Precisely," I replied, delighted that he was grasping the issue.

Bob's tone grew determined. "So if we lead by example and demonstrate CLEAR in our interactions, we can show others how to build a safer environment?"

"Totally, Bob! Leading by example is key. Our commitment to these principles will inspire others to follow. And by adhering to these principles, we set a standard for how we communicate and collaborate. It's a signal that we value a culture where everyone feels safe to speak up and contribute."

"But what happens when we have disagreements?" Bob asked, ever inquisitive.

"Ooh, excellent question! We need to rediscover the art of disagreement without turning it into a personal feud. These days, it seems we've forgotten how to debate ideas without attacking individuals. It's either complete agreement or you're labeled as intolerant. Inclusivity doesn't mean never questioning or debating. Maybe we can offer some guidance on navigating these waters."

"Yes, a set of guidelines would act like a compass, reminding everyone that respectful disagreement is not a personal attack."

I leaned in, ready to help craft these guidelines. "Let's start with a clear rule: When we disagree, we focus on the idea, not the person. No personal attacks whatsoever. Besides, we've carefully chosen our team through a rigorous interview process. They've already proven their capabilities and met our high standards."

Bob chimed in, his first few words overlapping mine in his eagerness. "It's good to restate the other person's argument in your own words, to show you've really understood them. That's the *R* in CLEAR—Repeating and reviewing points."

"We can't forget the *C* in CLEAR either. Curiosity, care, and open-mindedness should guide these debates. Approaching discussions with genuine curiosity and assuming positive intent allows us to focus on the issues rather than the individuals." I paused, letting the thought sink in. "When we come from a place of compassion, debates become less heated."

Eager to cement the idea, I added, "For curiosity and open-mindedness, active listening is key. People should listen actively to the other person and digest what they're saying. Most people tend to start formulating rebuttals while others are speaking. If you're busy crafting your response, you're not truly absorbing their viewpoint. We need to digest what's being said without prematurely formulating counterarguments. That's the essence of being truly curious and understanding."

"Indeed. It's essential to absorb the essence of the other person's perspective and words without hastily preparing responses."

"You're right. Disagreements often stem from our complex perspectives and experiences and the risks we're willing to take. It's not always easy to articulate every thought, especially when ideas are still forming. That's where the caring aspect comes in, allowing people to express themselves as they're able in that moment without the pressure of saying it perfectly."

"Quite," Bob said. "Encouraging people to speak their minds is essential. It fosters an environment where every voice is valued, regardless of their language skills or how polished their thoughts are. We also need to cultivate open-mindedness and curiosity that go beyond the surface. We seek to comprehend not just the words but the essence of someone's thoughts, their unique perspectives, and the influences shaping their viewpoint."

"Precisely. We assume positive intent and strive to understand the influences behind their words, not just the words themselves. Our goal is to engage in calm, constructive discussions that lead to deeper understanding. Sometimes their perspective sheds light on aspects we may have missed, and vice versa."

Bob mirrored my enthusiasm. "When we allow each person to express their perspective freely, we create a space that welcomes diverse opinions. It's not just about winning an argument; it's about embracing the richness of diverse voices."

"Totally! That's the *E* in CLEAR—Encourage everyone to contribute. It emphasizes the importance of expressing and valuing a diverse range of opinions, fostering an atmosphere where every voice is not only heard but genuinely valued for the unique perspective it brings."

"That's right," Bob said. "Encouraging diverse opinions is the very foundation of psychological safety, allowing every voice, no matter how unpopular, to be heard without fear of retribution. Imagine an environment where all voices could thrive, even those of the minority . . ."

I contemplated the implications of these principles in our meeting culture. "Indeed. So, before delving into sensitive topics, we can emphasize the importance of considering all viewpoints, assuring everyone that their input is not only valued but essential in shaping our decisions."

"Oh, Wendy," Bob said, his usual calm tone tinged with excitement. "These guidelines could truly equip our teams to navigate disagreements constructively, avoiding unproductive and potentially destructive confrontations."

As we continued, Bob's voice turned pensive. "What if it's not an outright attack but an unintended offense? How do we deal with it without undermining the safety that is built?"

"We need to approach this gently." I recalled scenarios where well-intended words or actions inadvertently caused harm, then continued. "It's about understanding the repercussions of what we say or do, even if no offense is meant."

Bob's voice was measured. "So, if someone's attempt at humor causes distress, the first step is acknowledging the discomfort it causes, even if unintended. If the speaker is unaware of their impact, facilitators should guide them delicately, either through a private conversation or a skillfully orchestrated group discussion."

"Absolutely. There's no one-size-fits-all approach. It depends on the context, but what's vital is both parties handling these instances with sensitivity, addressing them calmly and directly. It's about fostering mutual understanding, allowing us to navigate each other's perspectives with empathy and grace."

"By initiating these conversations, we not only help others comprehend different perspectives, but we also foster an environment of growth and understanding. Empathy—"

"Becomes the bridge between our diverse viewpoints," I said, finishing his thought.

PRO TIPS

- Going over the meeting agreement (abiding by the CLEAR method) at the beginning of every meeting may seem tedious, but it's crucial if you want people to speak up in the meeting and have a constructive discussion.

- After attendees have agreed to the meeting agreement, if at any point during the meeting one or more of those agreements is broken, it is the duty of the other attendees to stop the meeting and point that out, regardless of the offender's rank or title. Otherwise, the meeting agreement will become meaningless. Remember, it takes time to build psychological safety and trust, but it takes only a moment to destroy them.

- In decision-making meetings, when participants cannot agree to a decision, you can try a "good enough" or "I can live with this" type of decision, called the "Fist of Five" approach, to move the meeting forward.

  - Closed fist: No way! I'll block this!

  - One finger (index finger): I have major concerns.

  - Two fingers: I would like to discuss some minor issues.

- Three fingers: I'm not in total agreement, but I feel comfortable enough to let this proposal pass without further discussion.

- Four fingers: I think it's a good idea and will work for it.

- Five fingers: I love this! I'll champion it!

EXERCISE

When trying CLEAR, also prepare your response in case people are not adhering to the CLEAR agreement. What will you do or say? Write it down in advance. Make sure your response is CLEAR as well.

8.
FOSTERING
OPEN DIALOGUE

AS WE CONTINUED OUR DISCUSSION on the art of disagreement, Bob suddenly said, "Remember Vernā Myers' quote? Diversity is being invited to the party. Inclusion is being asked to dance. ™ When we provide a safe platform for individuals to express dissenting opinions, we're essentially extending that invitation. But it doesn't end there. The real essence lies in harnessing these diverse perspectives to construct something truly remarkable."

I responded enthusiastically. "Lovely quote. She says it quite eloquently. In arguments, people often focus on dominance and being right. But our aim should always be centered around collaborative problem-solving and finding the best possible solution. It's not about who is right."

"Exactly! By implementing these principles, we're not just managing disagreements, we're fostering respect and open communication, building a psychologically safe space where innovation can flourish."

"And by consistently modeling these practices, we cultivate an environment where these skills organically permeate the discussions. As facilitators lead by example, others can follow suit, each bringing their unique style to the table."

Without missing a beat, Bob asked, "Is there a way to regularly measure the psychological safety in our teams and meetings?"

"Absolutely!" I replied eagerly. "Dr. Amy Edmondson developed a survey with seven statements assessing the different dimensions of psychological safety we've been exploring: the celebration of diversity, the acceptance of risk and failure, the readiness to offer support within the team, and the openness of conversation."

"That sounds fascinating. Can we go through these statements?"

"Of course. Let's dive right in. Number one: It is difficult to ask other members of this team for help." I paused before continuing. "Number two: No one on this team would deliberately act in a way that undermines my efforts.

"Number three: Working with members of this team, my unique skills and talents are valued and utilized. Number four: People on this team sometimes reject others for being different. Please note that it's a reverse-worded statement, a clever trap for biases to reveal themselves."

Bob winced a little.

"You alright?" I asked.

"Yeah, go on." Bob said softly.

"Number five: If you make a mistake on this team, it is often held against you."

Bob groaned.

"Number six: It is safe to take a risk on this team. And number seven: Members of this team are able to bring up problems and tough issues."

I continued. "These statements aren't looking for simple 'true' or 'false' answers. Instead, they use a Likert Scale, allowing participants to express how strongly they agree or disagree. And watch for reverse-crafted statements like number four, which help us get a holistic grasp of our team dynamics."

"That's quite an elaborate approach. But wouldn't it be burdensome to administer this questionnaire after every single meeting?"

I paused, considering his point. "You're right. Gathering immediate responses after each meeting might not capture the true essence of team dynamics and could potentially lead to survey fatigue. Instead, we could implement this survey quarterly. That way, team members can provide candid feedback without feeling the pressure of immediate responses."

Bob's voice brightened. "I got it!" he exclaimed. "Why not use applications like email, Mentimeter, or Google Forms? It'll give people an easy way to chime in while keeping things anonymous."

"Brilliant," I said, pleased with his suggestion. "The technology side is important. But we also need someone to facilitate the team discussion afterward. A trusted third party could compute and analyze the survey responses and then guide the team through an open dialogue about strengths and weaknesses. It's hard to facilitate those conversations *and* be a participant at the same time."

"Compute the survey responses? I thought you just review people's answers and summarize them yourself."

"Oh, no! This isn't a normal survey," I explained. "The Likert Scale demands a more comprehensive approach. People rate their responses on a scale, usually from 'strongly disagree' to 'strongly agree.' This nuanced approach ensures feedback isn't just binary but encompasses the spectrum of feelings and experiences within the team. Therefore, responses need to be calculated and structured before analysis. It's a crucial step that often requires a specialized skill set to ensure accurate interpretation."

"That's interesting. So there's a precise methodology behind it. The process is more involved than I initially thought."

"Totally," I said. "It's essential to follow a systematic process, especially when dealing with the nuances of psychological safety. This meticulous approach ensures a thorough understanding of the team dynamics, allowing us to make well-informed decisions moving forward."

Bob spoke slowly, taking it all in. "I see. That does offer a comprehensive insight into the team's dynamics. But doing this once a quarter seems a bit . . . after the fact. Are there other steps we can take during or before meetings?"

Reflecting on our experiences, I replied thoughtfully. "We can start by modeling the right behaviors ourselves. At the start of each meeting, we should establish that our primary goal is to learn from one another, align on goals, and work cohesively toward our shared objectives. Curiosity and asking questions should always be encouraged."

"Go on," Bob prompted.

Building on my point, I stressed the importance of nurturing a culture of continuous learning and growth. "For example, when a team member encounters a setback or makes a mistake, I make it clear that it's perfectly alright. Mistakes and setbacks are a natural part of the learning process. What matters is how we learn from these experiences, prioritizing growth over assigning blame. I would then engage the team in reflective discussions about what adjustments we could make to prevent similar issues in the future."

"And don't forget about celebrating the wins! We should seize the opportunity to come together as a team and explore how we can replicate these triumphs and successes more broadly."

I chuckled. "I knew you wouldn't forget celebrating success-es! By incorporating these practices, we address survey concerns and foster an environment where team members feel safe taking risks and contributing openly, knowing that their ideas and con-cerns matter just as much as their successes."

"This all makes sense when we can see the issues right there in the meeting," Bob said slowly. "But what about when people are afraid to bring up bad news in the first place?" He paused, his voice softening with concern. "Like last week during my one-on-one with Maria, I noticed she was fidgeting. She was clearly upset but she was afraid to tell me what was wrong."

"Oh? What happened?" I asked eagerly.

"It took a lot of patient coaxing before she finally opened up about some problems her team was facing. She felt really stuck."

"That must have been tricky," I said. "If you don't mind sharing, and if it doesn't betray any confidences, how did you get her to open up?"

"Oh, I don't mind," Bob replied. "I told her I noticed some-thing was bugging her and that no matter what, I wouldn't blame her, even if it was something I didn't like. I told her I'm here for her and together we'll figure things out."

"I like what you told her, Bob," I interjected. "You empa-thized with her and told her your response in advance. That must have been reassuring for her."

As I reflected on what Bob said, his words struck a chord, evoking memories of similar instances where voicing concerns felt insurmountable. Sympathizing with Maria's predicament, I nod-ded, forgetting that Bob couldn't see me. "We can try to model transparency ourselves when we have tough news to share," I proposed. "But realistically, we can't demonstrate that vulnerability consistently."

I pondered the intricacies of building trust within a team dynamic. Tapping my pen on the table, I mulled over strategies to encourage a culture of openness. Then a spark of inspiration ignited within me and I sat up straighter. "You mentioned you noticed she was fidgeting. That's empathy on your part, being able to see someone is distressed. Taking time to relate to her and listening without judgment helped create that safety for her to open up. This approach also helps create safety for people to ask for help instead of keeping things bottled up."

"Transparency and empathy! That's the key!" Bob exclaimed. His voice grew more animated as he continued. "And it ties right back to Dr. Edmondson's first statement: It is difficult to ask other members of this team for help. Transparency and empathy help people feel comfortable asking for help and voicing concerns."

"You got it, Bob!" I was thrilled that we both understood the crucial link between empathy, transparency, and psychological safety. As we wrapped up our conversation, I knew that this was just the beginning of a new chapter in our team's journey toward more productive and fruitful collaborations.

PRO TIPS

- When the answers from the seven statements by Dr. Amy Edmondson come back not as positive as you'd like, I highly recommend you hire a trusted third-party facilitator (or someone within the company if they are trained) to facilitate a team discussion. The facilitator would help the team learn how to have a dialogue around strengths and weaknesses and how to take the next steps. It's really hard to facilitate those kinds of conversations and be one of the participants.

- Other than the quarterly survey of those seven statements, I recommend doing a quick retrospective at the end of each meeting (no more than two minutes) to see if the meeting was conducted according to the meeting agreement that was agreed upon at the start of the meeting. This is a quick pulse check and reinforces how the attendees want the meeting to be run.

- Transparency and empathy are crucial to establish a safe environment (as Bob demonstrated with Maria). In order to empathize and be transparent, you will need to have good listening skills. At a bare minimum, stop trying to process things in your head or thinking of how to respond when the other person is talking.

- There's much more to becoming a good listener. (By the way, active listening is only one of the skills you need.) If you're serious about improving your listening abilities and becoming a truly good listener, I recommend exploring my self-paced The Power of Listening online course: https://munwaic.com/online-courses/the-power-of-listening/ (discount code: Wendy).

EXERCISE

Use the seven statements by Dr. Amy Edmondson to evaluate if safety was indeed achieved in your meetings:

1. It is difficult to ask other members of this team for help.

2. No one on this team would deliberately act in a way that undermines my efforts.

3. Working with members of this team, my unique skills and talents are valued and utilized.

4. People on this team sometimes reject others for being different.

5. If you make a mistake on this team, it is often held against you.

6. It is safe to take a risk on this team.

7. Members of this team are able to bring up problems and tough issues.

Before leaving the topic of psychological safety, let's spend some time reflecting as another exercise. Ponder the following questions.

1. What was the result from those seven statements by Dr. Amy Edmondson? Does going through the survey alone change how people behave in the meetings and how meetings are conducted? It should! It should at least lead to amending the meeting agreements.

2. Have you tried modeling transparency and empathy? What other things can you do to ensure the meeting agreements carry over to the day-to-day interactions between colleagues?

3. How do you react when people make mistakes? How do people react when you make a mistake? Do you look for someone to blame or do you look for learnings to be gleaned? Remember, when there is psychological safety, people will support each other. They are willing to show vulnerability, suggest new ideas, flag sensitive issues, admit mistakes, and debate constructively. That's how we get engaging teams, and that's how teams can start to become high-performing.

4. As we all know, leaders' actions have a wider impact to the organization. So are there any situations where you, as a leader, might have flubbed modeling safe behavior? Now rewrite those situations using the techniques described in chapters 6, 7, and 8 for better outcomes.

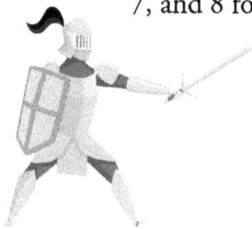

9.
AN ENGAGING
PROPOSITION

THE NEXT DAY, I saw a Slack message from Bob. "Wendy, I think we're ready for the facilitation training with all the materials we've identified. Let's start putting the invitation together and get it scheduled!"

"Not so fast, Bob!" I quickly typed back. "Remember some time ago, we stumbled upon a treasure trove of suggestions on how to turn lackluster meetings into engaging ones?"

Bob's three gray dots blinked reassuringly, and soon his reply came through. "Ah, right! Thanks for reminding me! We did chat about those in passing. We better jot down all of those ideas, the good, the bad, and the quirky."

"Good idea," I replied. "Let's gather them up and give them a thorough once-over. Hey, why don't we hop on a call? It'll be quicker to hash this out verbally."

With Bob's agreement, I initiated the audio call. As soon as the connection clicked into place, I dove right in. "Alright, I got a blank document open. Let me share that doc with you."

"Thanks. I am in the doc," Bob said. "Let's kick off with the popular advice of having a crystal clear agenda before the meeting."

"Mm-hmm. But as we discussed, a mere agenda isn't enough for a truly engaging and productive meeting."

"Precisely," Bob agreed, his tone measured. "That's the bare minimum."

"Ooh, here's another common one," I chimed in, my fingers dancing across the keys. "Ensuring there's a list of action items after each meeting for people to follow up on."

"Also useful, but insufficient," Bob responded quickly. "We talked about how meeting facilitators can't be the 'traffic cops' to ensure follow-through. Instead, we need to inspire people to own those action items and follow up themselves!"

I chuckled at his choice of words. "Inspire them?" I teased playfully.

"Absolutely! We need to make those tasks appealing by connecting them to something meaningful or beneficial," Bob said.

"Ah, yes!" I exclaimed, the memory clicking into place. "That ties into our chat about appealing to people's motivations. Inspire! You're funny, Bob." I chuckled again.

As our brainstorming continued, I brought up another popular meeting tactic. "Okay, what about icebreakers? I'm partial to using them to start meetings in a lighthearted manner."

"Ah, icebreakers," Bob replied, a touch of dry humor in his voice. "My eternal favorite! But let's consider their real purpose and value."

I pondered for a moment. "Well, icebreakers engage people lightly at the very start. They set the tone, infusing the room with an energetic mood, especially when we know the meeting might cover some weighty topics. They provide that metaphorical breather, something easygoing."

"True," Bob affirmed. "But instead of just any random ice-breaker, what if we aligned them with the meeting's main topic?"

"Oh!" I snapped my fingers. "Like that word game we did recently! For our meeting related to performance review, we used *performance* and asked people to make new words from its letters. It was fun and it got everyone focused on that word from the beginning."

"Subliminal messaging, you could say," Bob quipped.

We both chuckled, then Bob turned serious again. "The key is to keep icebreakers short and sweet and not take away time from the real meeting," he cautioned.

"Absolutely. I've seen meetings derail because the icebreaker was too entertaining and ate into discussion time."

Bob summed it up neatly. "Icebreakers: short, light, and connected to the meeting's purpose."

"But sometimes it's not just about the direct connection to the meeting purpose. They can also help foster stronger connections between team members over time."

Bob's curiosity sparked to life. "Oh? Explain, please."

"How much time do you have, Bob?" I teased before diving in. "We know icebreakers as 'warm-up' acts, breaking down barriers, getting folks comfortable talking and interacting with each other. That sets the stage for better communication down the road."

"Go on," Bob encouraged.

"But did you know that effective icebreakers help team members discover common ground? Recognizing shared experiences, values, hobbies, or even just silly things like favorite foods can create bonds. And then there are these interactive icebreakers.

They encourage teamwork and collaboration, helping to build trust from the start."

"Hmm . . .," Bob mused.

"But wait, there's more!" I exclaimed. "Icebreakers can make team members relate more personally. Team members become more than just colleagues—they become real people with light-hearted facts, stories, and goals. That helps them start seeing each other as multidimensional individuals."

I continued my crusade. "And the silly ones? The ones that make you chuckle or cringe? They're the secret sauce. Laughter creates a positive environment, reduces stress, and sparks chemistry. This leads to greater cohesiveness within a team."

Bob listened intently as I tied it all together.

I took a breath, ready for my grand finale. "So thoughtfully planned icebreakers aren't mere games. Over time, they help a team get to know each other, build trust, relate in meaningful ways, and create a positive and open atmosphere. This strengthens those interpersonal bonds so fundamental to an effective, cohesive, and productive team down the road."

There was a moment of silence before Bob spoke. "Wow! I had no idea that thoughtfully planned icebreakers have this many long-term benefits. You've opened my eyes to a whole new perspective!"

Without skipping a beat, Bob transitioned smoothly. "What's your take on mid-meeting energizers?" he asked, his tone carrying a hint of excitement. "I've heard they can reignite the spark during long sessions. Some say that meetings over an hour should include a brief break with an energizing activity."

I imagined him leaning in, eager for my response. "Well,"

I began, "our minds do benefit from occasional breaks to regain focus. A brief, energizing activity in a lengthy meeting can break the monotony and offer everyone a chance to recharge."

"Not quite," he corrected. "While energizers can provide short physical or mental breaks, they aren't about breaking up the monotony of long meetings; they're about giving our brains a breather. This way, participants can redirect their attention and return more engaged. Plus, energizers get people moving, laughing, and interacting. This is especially beneficial in long meetings, boosting participants' energy levels and sustaining their interest."

"I see where you're coming from. But I have mixed feelings about energizers. What revitalizes one person might not have the same effect on another," I said slowly. "And there's a critical aspect you may have overlooked."

"Oh? What am I missing?" Bob asked.

I jumped at the chance to explain. "As you said, energizers get people moving and engaged. But it's crucial to consider diverse personalities, preferences, and physical abilities. Many facilitators impose energizers from their own standpoint, often neglecting attendees who might be less extroverted or physically capable."

Bob's thoughtful "hmm" told me he was really listening, and I continued. "It's a bit risky to assume everyone's just like us."

"I hadn't thought of that," Bob admitted. "That's a crucial point we absolutely can't overlook in our meetings and training sessions!"

I nodded and shared a memory that had stuck with me. "I remember a facilitator leading an energizer involving shoulder movements. One participant confided that he couldn't participate because of recent shoulder surgery."

A pang of empathy resurfaced as I recounted the man's discomfort. "He said it would have been really painful for him. It struck me then that we must always factor in people's physical limitations, even ones we can't see. This guy didn't have a sling or anything; there was no way to know just by looking at him."

"That's a critical point about inclusivity, Wendy," Bob echoed, his voice warm with understanding. "For physical energizers, we could always provide options—move your arms, stretch your legs, nod your head, and even something as simple as moving your eyes!"

I immediately swayed my eyes from side to side. "Well, that little eye workout did jolt me back into focus a bit!"

"See! Or we could introduce quick breathing exercises as energizers, something that doesn't demand intricate movements."

My fingers drummed lightly on my desk as I thought aloud. "The key is giving people choices so no one feels excluded while effectively communicating the intended objective."

"Exactly!" Then, with a mischievous tone, he added, "Maybe I'll suggest a 'mouth movement' energizer at our next meeting. You know, involving eating something!"

We both erupted into laughter, enjoying the lighthearted banter.

"But Wendy," Bob persisted, "energizers really do liven things up! They get people laughing, playing, and connecting. Don't you think that would help us all see each other in a more relaxed light? That can foster connections among participants who might not interact much during the formal parts of the meeting."

I mulled over his words. I had to admit, Bob's enthusiasm for injecting some fun into meetings was contagious. "You know what, you've convinced me! Energizers could be great. The key is to pick the right activities, considering the diversity of the attendees—their personalities, preferences, physical capabilities, and even their cultural backgrounds and languages. We need to read the room and be ready to make last-minute changes."

"You nailed it! I'm thrilled you're finally on board with this."

PRO TIPS

- Not all meetings need icebreakers and energizers. Make sure those activities are purposeful.

- No matter how fun icebreakers and energizers are, they are not the goals of the meeting unless it's a socializing event. So make sure those activities are time-bound and do not bleed into the actual meeting itself.

- If the meeting is over an hour long, it is a good guideline to have a short break (e.g., five minutes) for every forty-five to fifty minutes.

- As a facilitator or meeting host, you shouldn't assume your meeting participants are like you. So make sure you consider all the aspects that we mentioned in this chapter when planning icebreakers and energizers.

EXERCISE

For your next meeting, plan and write down the icebreakers and energizers you'll use based on the teachings from this chapter. Also, specify how long you intend each activity to last.

10.
BEHIND THE SCENES
OF SEAMLESS

AS BOB AND I CONTINUED OUR AUDIO CALL, veering into the intricacies of effective meeting management, Bob's voice took on a note of urgency. "We can't afford to overlook our guidance on attendee locations," he said, as if a sudden realization had just struck him.

I wracked my brain trying to piece together what he meant, then said, "Wait, what exactly are you referring to?" I was eager to connect the dots.

Bob, ever composed, quickly clarified. "We need to emphasize the importance of having additional facilitators to ensure the smooth running of fully remote or hybrid meetings. We don't want to be affected by anything that takes away time from the agenda. In a fully remote setup, the facilitator might not have the capacity to handle technical issues or manage logistical tasks like breakout rooms or screen sharing, all while steering the meeting. Bringing in a co-facilitator could help balance the workload, allowing the primary facilitator to focus on creating an engaging and impactful experience."

A spark of excitement lit up inside me as I listened intently. "Of course! That's a crucial point! We should make it clear that for fully remote setups, there should be at least two facilitators—one to run the meeting and another to handle any technical and logistical issues. That way, the primary facilitator can focus on making the meeting truly impactful."

"And for hybrid setups, it gets even more complex."

"Three facilitators!" I bursted out, unable to contain my excitement. "One serving as the primary facilitator overseeing the meeting flow, and two others handling the technical and logistical aspects—one focusing on the remote participants and the other stationed at the physical location managing things on-site." I imagined the seamless teamwork behind the scenes.

"Exactly," Bob responded. "It's crucial to recognize that these technical facilitators aren't just IT support. They're integral to the meeting's design. So when the primary facilitator sits down to design a meeting, the technical facilitators should be involved from the start, collaborating on the design."

"That's a great point! We should emphasize that all facilitators have a common script outlining everyone's role during the meeting. Plus, ample rehearsal time is key. Practicing beforehand helps them find the ideal rhythm of the event, so even if unexpected glitches pop up, they'll be adept at seamlessly handling the situation, ensuring a smooth and uninterrupted experience for the attendees."

"Absolutely!" Bob said. "The goal is to ensure the meeting runs smoothly for the attendees, no matter what happens behind the scenes. Remember those times we used to rehearse endlessly for those complex meetings? We'd run through the script over and over, just to make sure we were fully prepared."

I smiled as memories of those intense prep sessions flooded back. "I remember it well. I'm so glad we're incorporating these crucial guidelines to ensure multifacilitator teams have a solid foundation for success."

Then a new thought struck me, interrupting the flow of our conversation. "But wait . . . if people are calling meetings only for things like problem-solving, brainstorming, and occasional decision-making, like we suggested, and use your six-point framework, won't the meetings be smaller? With fewer attendees, especially if they're technical folks, couldn't they manage with just one facilitator?"

There was a brief pause as Bob mulled over my point. "Perhaps . . .," he said hesitantly. "But we have to remember, seamless flow for attendees is paramount. I've been in too many meetings where the facilitator got bogged down with technical issues or let problems linger because they were too focused on facilitation. In both cases, the quality of the meeting suffered."

I nodded, recognizing the truth in his words. "You're right. That's a really good point."

As the conversation ebbed, a sudden realization jolted me into an active train of thought. "Considering our upcoming facilitation training, are we leaning toward a fully remote setup or perhaps a hybrid model?" I mulled over the logistics that would inevitably follow. "We'll need to strategize the roles accordingly. Naturally, you and I would take up the mantle of facilitators, with the technical responsibilities to be allocated later."

I paused, allowing the idea to settle before continuing. "In the case of a hybrid setup, it's imperative we enlist a third facilitator specifically to oversee the technical intricacies at the physical venue," I added, verbalizing the complexities that a hybrid model inevitably introduced.

"I believe, or rather, you believe, Wendy, that it's time to loop in our ever-busy boss, Peter, and get his input on the matter first," he quipped, his words laced with a subtle hint of amusement.

An exaggerated sigh escaped my lips. "Oh, why do you always 'voluntell' me for these things?!" I protested, a hint of jest softening my irritation.

"Because you're undeniably the best at it!" he countered warmly, his tone filled with mischief. "Off you go now, Wendy, and have that chat with Peter. Let's get this training on the calendar!"

Shaking my head in playful resignation, I took a moment to gather my thoughts before replying, "Alright, alright! I suppose it's time for me to circle back to Peter, not only about the logistics for this training but also about the matters concerning psychological safety. Plus, there's the ongoing dialogue with the video production team. I'll send Peter a message right after we hang up. Hopefully, he'll reply soon. Then we can get this training scheduled."

"Sounds like a plan," Bob said. "Let me know how it goes."

We ended our call, and I immediately reached out to Peter, asking for some time to discuss these topics. To my surprise, he responded almost immediately with his availability.

And so, at the agreed-upon time, I took a deep breath before initiating the video call with my boss.

"Hi, Peter. Thanks for taking the time to meet." I greeted him with an upbeat tone as his face appeared on my screen. "I wanted to follow up on our last discussion about the issues the video production team is having."

Peter's brow furrowed with concern as he acknowledged, "Yes, it's been quite a struggle. Did you figure out what's at the root of the issue?"

Eager to jump in, I said, "I delved deeper into the matter, spending considerable time speaking with the team, observing their meetings, and brainstorming with Bob." I leaned forward, excited to convey the insights we had unearthed. "The crux of the problem lies in a lack of psychological safety within the team."

A flicker of recognition crossed Peter's face as he leaned in. "You mentioned the term *psychological safety* before. What does that mean again?"

With an earnest enthusiasm, I launched into a concise yet comprehensive explanation, drawing from Modern Agile's CLEAR framework and Dr. Amy Edmonson's expert views. I painted a picture of an environment where team members feel safe to express dissenting opinions, take calculated risks, and voice concerns without fearing any retribution.

"Psychological safety acts as the bedrock for fostering effective collaboration," I emphasized, hoping to convey the significance of this concept. "Without it, people may hold back concerns, which prevents teams from identifying and solving problems, leaving ideas and issues unexplored, and the team's potential remains untapped."

Peter leaned back in his chair with a contemplative expression. "I see. So what you're suggesting is that bolstering psychological safety could be the key to unraveling the other intricacies plaguing the video team."

"Exactly." I felt a sense of relief, gratified that he was following along. "There are certain measures we can implement to cultivate this, both within the confines of our meetings and beyond."

As I explained the intricacies of fostering a psychologically safe environment, Peter nodded thoughtfully, his eyes fixed on the screen. I emphasized the importance of actively seeking input from quieter team members and creating a nonjudgmental atmosphere for questions and concerns, and I highlighted the influential role of his demeanor and communication style in shaping the team's dynamics.

Peter paused. "Hmm . . . I don't think I intentionally pull rank in meetings, but I just realized that my tendency to critique may have inadvertently created a barrier," he acknowledged. "Perhaps my approach has been undermining the very psychological safety we're trying to build."

I nodded sympathetically, understanding his concern. "It's a common pitfall, even without pulling rank. Bob and I have been discussing these nuances extensively, and we're gearing up to address them in our upcoming facilitation training workshop."

As Peter expressed his enthusiasm for the upcoming workshop, a sense of validation washed over me. It was heartening to witness his genuine interest in the initiative and his willingness to actively participate in fostering a more inclusive and supportive work environment.

"I'm thrilled you're on board, Peter," I responded, meeting his warm smile. "Your support means a lot to both Bob and I. We're looking forward to making a tangible difference here."

Peter opened his mouth to reply, but his expression quickly shifted to a frown. "I'm sorry, Wendy," he said abruptly, his tone shifting. "I have to go. Something urgent just came up. Let's continue this discussion later."

"Of course," I replied quickly, understanding the sudden change of plans. "I'll find a time on your calendar for us to continue our discussion."

PRO TIPS

- Make sure you have at least two facilitators for all remote meetings and three for hybrid meetings. You may be able to get by with just one facilitator if the meeting is small and the attendees are technical. But remember, the goal is to maintain a seamless flow for attendees and make sure the quality of the meeting does not suffer.

- Make sure all facilitators work together to design the meeting and build the script together. The tech facilitator is not IT support.

- Co-creating the script doesn't ensure the meeting will run smoothly. Make sure to practice the script before the meeting begins.

- Before the meeting begins, make sure you have time for technical checks with all facilitators to ensure all the elements are in place and ready to function as you expect.

- Make sure you involve your executives in improving your meetings and the psychological safety of your teams in and outside of meetings, especially when the executives' behavior, actions, and words have significant impact. Follow Wendy and Bob's example of involving their boss, Peter, early on in the process, helping him learn and grow as well.

- It is not uncommon that executives get called away in the middle of a conversation. Be flexible and make sure you follow up.

EXERCISE

1. Are you running a remote or hybrid meeting? If so, who are the additional facilitators?

2. As Wendy mentioned, all facilitators should have a common script outlining everyone's role during the meeting, so it's time to complete the script, together with all co-facilitators! From the previous exercises, you have started planning how to run the meeting (i.e., facilitate) so that the meeting will satisfy the metrics that are outlined in chapter 5. Use what I outlined in this chapter to finish building your meeting script.

   a. Five to ten minutes: get everyone aligned (review the asynchronous pre-work to get them in the right mindset).

   b. Two to three minutes: Quick one-word check-in.

   c. Two to three minutes: go over team agreements on how to behave using CLEAR.

   d. What, if any, icebreakers are you going to use? How long does each one last?

   e. Run the agenda (per your design in chapter 5) in an inclusive and engaging manner for all participants, whether remote or in person. Don't just call out each agenda item. You can make it more engaging by using techniques like Liberating Structures for each of your agenda items.

f. Is your meeting over an hour? If so, have you scheduled enough breaks?

g. Are you planning to use energizing activities? If so, what energizers and for how long?

h. Run the agenda.

i. End the meeting:

    i. How much time are you going to give everyone to reflect on the work, celebrate the progress, and translate it to actionable next steps?

    ii. How do you plan to do a quick alignment check to ensure everyone departs on the same page? (Review chapter 5 for suggestions.)

    iii. Do you want to quickly gather feedback on how the team behaves regarding the team agreement? (Review chapter 8 for suggestions.)

    iv. Will you celebrate any successes / meeting goals achieved?

11.
CALENDAR CONQUERED

A FEW DAYS HAD PASSED since our last discussion, but Peter and I were finally able to resume our dialogue via another video call.

"Wendy, I owe you an apology for what happened last time," Peter began, his voice sincere. "And thank you for being so understanding and flexible."

I gave him a reassuring nod, urging him to continue.

"So, where were we?" he asked.

He rubbed his chin thoughtfully as I reminded him of the topics we'd covered.

"Ah yes, psychological safety. It's clearly been an overlooked issue on our teams." He leaned back in his chair, his brow furrowed. "And I understand the importance of leading by example. If my actions are hindering the progress, I trust you and Bob to steer me in the right direction during our meetings. It's all about that real-time feedback, isn't it? We learn as we go."

I smiled, appreciating his receptiveness. "Absolutely, Peter. Bob and I are more than willing to provide that guidance. Constructive feedback is pivotal in our growth process."

Peter's warm chuckle filtered through the screen. "I have no doubt that you both will handle it tactfully." He flashed me a grin. "You seem well prepared for the workshop. Whether you want it completely virtual or a blend of virtual and in person, the choice is yours. I'll back you up in any way I can."

"Thank you, Peter," I replied sincerely, grateful for his unwavering support. "Your flexibility means a lot, and it will certainly make a significant impact on the success of this endeavor."

I ended the call with a final nod and a heartfelt smile. Then I reflected on my exchange with Peter. A sense of relief washed over me, mingling with anticipation. With Peter's backing and guidance, I was confident that Bob and I could truly make a difference. I looked forward to reconnecting with Bob to discuss the final touches for our much-anticipated training session.

My fingertips danced across the keyboard as I shared the positive outcome of my conversation, relaying the highlights of my discussion with our boss. I hoped to convey the full extent of Peter's newfound enthusiasm for our cause. "Bob, great news! I talked to Peter, and he's fully on board with us on the psychological safety front," I messaged, my excitement practically jumping off the screen.

Moments later, Bob's response appeared, his bitmoji exuding his trademark enthusiasm. "That's fantastic! What's the scoop? What did he say?"

Grinning mischievously, I couldn't resist a playful tease. "Well, brace yourself, my friend. Peter has an action item specially reserved for you," I wrote back cheekily. "He's counting on you to point out any time he does something in meetings that negatively impacts psychological safety."

A series of laughing emojis from Bob's end told me he was taking it in good humor. "Oh joy, thanks for throwing me into the fire!" he quipped.

Chuckling to myself, I replied, "Come on, you know you love a good challenge. Besides, Peter did emphasize how much he values our input in his learning process."

"Touché," Bob messaged back, his tone laced with good-natured banter. "I'm all in for fostering a more inclusive and supportive environment, so count me in for this feedback mission."

I felt a swell of pride at his commitment. "That's the spirit! We're in this together," I typed with an added sense of camaraderie. "Funny how Peter seemed so sure we'd be excited to provide him with some insightful feedback."

Bob's bitmoji popped up again, a virtual grin plastered across his face. "Looks like our boss has us pegged," he remarked.

Eager to share more positive news, I continued. "And that's not all. Peter also gave us the green light for our facilitation training workshop. He's leaving it up to us to decide if we want to go fully remote or opt for a hybrid approach."

Bob's bitmoji looked pensive. "Hmm, hybrid could be good because hybrid is a lot more complicated than fully remote or completely in person. The techniques that people learn in hybrid actually translate easier in fully remote or fully in-person meetings. It'll also allow us to practice the techniques in a blended setting. How about we schedule it at least two weeks from today? This way, we have some time to drum up interest with people. It'll also allow people to create some space on their calendars for this training as well as prepare for the pre-work we will have them do."

I found myself a little confused. "Pre-work? I thought we're not asking for any pre-work, but instead use the first ten minutes to ask what people's expectations are."

"Ah, that's right! That's what we discussed before. But let's think through this a bit. Preparing them with some preliminary work could set the stage for a more engaged and fruitful session."

"Hmmm, alright. And you make a compelling point about the benefits of a hybrid approach," I typed, eager to contribute to the brainstorming process. "It allows us to demonstrate the techniques in a realistic setting, paving the way for a smoother transition in various meeting formats."

I paused for a moment to consider the logistics, then typed, "Scheduling it at least two weeks from now sounds ideal. We'll have ample time to generate interest and ensure everyone has the necessary bandwidth for the training."

"Absolutely. Giving people enough notice is key. We don't want to spring this on them at the last minute. But we also don't want to stretch it out too far."

His acknowledgment of the importance of timing resonated with me. "Exactly, no more than three weeks. We need to strike that balance," I affirmed. "And roping in another skilled facilitator to join our team could definitely add more depth and perspective to the training. It'll ensure we cover all the crucial aspects thoroughly."

"Definitely," Bob replied promptly. "Having another facilitator on board will enable us to distribute the workload effectively, enhancing the overall impact of the workshop. So let's set the date three weeks from now. This should give us ample time to scout for the right collaborator and synchronize our efforts seamlessly."

A surge of satisfaction swept over me as I considered how far we had come. "It's all falling into place," I remarked with a sense of optimism, my smile widening at the thought of the possibilities ahead. "Let's catch up later to hash out the finer details and get the ball rolling."

Bob's reassuring thumbs-up emoji flashed on the screen, re-affirming our shared commitment to this mission. "Absolutely, partner! This workshop is poised to revolutionize the way people work together here."

Settling back in my chair, I couldn't help but feel a sense of pride. With Peter's unwavering support, Bob's invaluable partner-ship, and our collective determination, we were poised to make a significant impact on the collaborative dynamics within our company. This training workshop marked just the beginning of a transformative journey ahead.

Over the following months, Bob and I put our proposed changes into action. The training we conducted was well received, yet the transformation didn't happen overnight. Breaking the in-grained habits of traditional meeting scheduling proved to be a challenge. Old habits die hard, as they say. It wasn't unexpected since altering the approach to meetings meant reshaping the en-tire company culture. Company culture encompasses how we col-laborate, think, and behave; the actions we take to achieve goals; and the habits and beliefs supporting those goals.

Changing this culture posed difficulties because meetings had been the collaborative norm for over a century. Concepts like asynchronous work required time for understanding and imple-mentation. But Bob and I were determined. We worked tirelessly with each team, helping them to transition to the novel thinking and practices we introduced. It was an uphill battle at times. More than once, I questioned whether our efforts would ever take hold. It was hard work.

Fortunately, we had the steadfast support of Peter, our senior executive. He recognized that shifting the culture was critical for the company's future success. Gradually, like a seedling breaking through the earth, a shift in the meeting culture began to emerge. People started viewing collaborations through a different lens. Meetings were no longer merely scheduled; when they did occur, they were focused and productive.

Throughout the company, Bob and I gained recognition for our role in teaching effective meeting strategies and spearheading the movement to reclaim time from unnecessary meetings. We became trailblazers changing the way we worked, transforming the way we collaborate, and reshaping the company culture to better suit the post-pandemic world. Our colleagues expressed their gratitude, and there was a collective sigh of relief as our once-cluttered calendars began to clear. It was a victory not just for me but for the entire department. We had successfully cut down the number of meetings and made room for more meaning-ful work. And as for Peter, he had become a convert to the cause, valuing the newfound efficiency as much as the rest of us.

With a lighter calendar and a sense of accomplishment, I knew we could finally get back to what really mattered—doing our jobs effectively and making a real impact. And if anyone dared to schedule an unnecessary meeting, they'd have to reckon with me, Wendy the Meeting Slayer.

It seemed like the tide had finally turned in our battle against never-ending meetings.

PRO TIPS

As Wendy's story concludes, I want to share four final important points:

- Hybrid is the hardest. If your company has offices/hubs in multiple locations, then you're in a permanent hybrid environment. So learning how to plan and facilitate a hybrid meeting well will make your fully remote or completely in-person meetings a lot easier. Or, take my advice: if one person is remote, everyone is remote. Then you'll have only a fully remote meeting instead of a hybrid one.

- Don't be dismayed if change takes time. Getting people to think differently about meetings is a long journey because you're changing the company culture. Lizzie Benton, a culture specialist, uses the metaphor of a high-performing athlete who wants to achieve a gold medal. Everything that they do in order to achieve that gold medal is their own culture. Remember, culture encompasses how we think and behave, the actions we take to achieve goals, and the habits and beliefs supporting those goals. High-performing athletes work on their mindset and their beliefs, their habits and their behaviors, and all of those various aspects that enable them to reach the goal of achieving a gold medal. For over a century, meetings have been the way to collaborate. It is how people work together. It has become a habit even though our environments have changed. So start small, one meeting at a time, like Wendy. With persistence and perseverance, and the support of colleagues and executives, the culture will change.

- Celebrate every step of the journey. Bob frequently emphasizes celebration, whether it's for progress, wins, successes, or goal achievement. This mindset isn't just for meetings or projects; it's essential for your journey too. As you heard in Wendy's account, this path is challenging and full of obstacles. That's why it's crucial to celebrate the small victories along the way. These moments of recognition will keep you motivated and help you persevere through the long journey ahead.

- You might have noticed Wendy's bubbly demeanor and think you need to be just as outgoing to effectively champion change. That's a misconception. Anyone can champion change, regardless of their personality. What's important is that people feel your passion and excitement for the change you're advocating. Would it surprise you to learn that Wendy is actually an introvert? And despite his calm demeanor, Bob is also a key player in this dynamic duo.

EXERCISE

Before we leave, let's spend some time reflecting as the final exercise.

1. Do you have anyone partnering with you on this journey? If you're in senior leadership, are you the executive champion driving this initiative across your department or even the entire company? If not, could you be? Who can be the Wendy or Bob in your teams to help you? If you're not an executive, do you have a senior management champion? Having an executive advocate can significantly bolster your endeavors. So find someone who shares your vision for a more collaborative workplace and has the influence to help make it a reality.

2. Do you have fewer meetings? When you do have live, synchronous meetings, do they meet the meeting metrics I outlined in chapter 5? If not, what experiments can you try to change that?

3. If you have been doing all the exercises from the past chapters, you are well on your way in this long journey. What wins or progress have you achieved (big or small)? Did you take the time to write them down and celebrate, no matter how small? You should!

EPILOGUE

TEN MONTHS LATER

Eager to share the latest breakthrough with Bob, I practically sprinted back to my desk after the video production team meeting. I eagerly launched Slack, hoping to convey the exciting news to my ever-supportive colleague. "Bob! You there?"

The screen remained blank for a few agonizing moments before the familiar three dots appeared, signaling Bob was crafting his reply. Finally, his message appeared. "Hey Wendy, I'm here just working on some stuff. What's going on?"

I could barely contain my excitement as I typed back rapidly. "You'll never guess what I just learned! Remember our work with the video team a while back, focusing on bolstering psychological safety and engagement?"

"Of course, how could I forget? Their engagement scores were plummeting on the last survey."

A wide grin spread across my face as I prepared to share the positive news. "Well, brace yourself for some good news! The latest survey results just came in, and there's been a significant upswing across the board for that very team! It's incredible to see the impact of our efforts materialize!"

"That's absolutely fantastic!" Bob's genuine excitement was palpable, even through text. "Perhaps they could serve as a shining example for other teams, a testament to what can be achieved through focused efforts on boosting psychological safety."

"I was thinking the same thing! We need these success stories to inspire and guide other teams in their journey toward improvement." The sense of achievement warmed my spirit.

Bob replied, "It's really great to see that work paying dividends. Hey, speaking of dividends, have you noticed we actually have time to work now?"

His astute observation drew a chuckle from me. "It's refreshing to have some breathing space now, isn't it? Our calendars aren't suffocatingly crammed anymore. It's a relief to witness the tangible impact of our training reflected in the newfound room to actually focus on work. Though there are still a few teams that need some reminders and guidance on how to think about meetings and what collaborations actually mean."

"Cut yourself some slack, Wendy. The progress we're seeing across the company is proof that our hard work is paying off."

Letting out a contemplative sigh, I typed my reply. "I know, patience is indeed a virtue I am learning to embrace. We've certainly made significant strides, but the path ahead still demands our continued commitment."

Bob's virtual avatar reappeared, accompanied by the familiar typing indicator. "Absolutely. Cultural shifts don't happen overnight. But we're making headway, and we'll keep at it."

Acknowledging his wisdom, I responded with a renewed sense of determination. "Yes, you're right. Regular reinforcement of our training, especially for new team members, will be crucial in sustaining this positive momentum."

I took a moment to reflect on Peter's subtle yet profound change in his approach. "Have you noticed how much Peter has evolved? His influence seems to be permeating among the other senior executives too."

Bob's response was swift and echoed my sentiments. "Absolutely. I also heard rumblings that Peter and the rest of the executives are contemplating rolling back the return-to-office mandate. They're thinking of letting teams decide for themselves when to go into the office based on their collaboration requirements."

The news left me momentarily startled; my eyebrows arched in surprise. It was a bold move, albeit one laden with potential risks. I mulled over the implications and carefully crafted my response. "It's a significant shift. And I worry about the potential challenges with new hires. They might not be attuned to our culture or the underlying principles driving our strategies. This could inadvertently jeopardize the very psychological safety we've worked so hard to foster."

"You're right. It's crucial that we incorporate this into our onboarding process. New team members need to understand the 'why' behind our practices and the outcomes we strive for, grounded in the company's core values. It's the cornerstone of preserving our strong culture, especially our commitment to psychological safety."

I took a moment to savor a sip of tea, then wrote, "Absolutely! Onboarding will play a pivotal role in upholding our ethos, particularly as we continue to expand our workforce. But this will undoubtedly translate into a significant project. We should definitely sync up with Peter before diving into this venture."

"Before you say it, Wendy, consider yourself 'voluntold'! LOL," he quipped, punctuating his words with a rolling-on-the-floor-laughing emoji.

I chuckled at his playful remark and couldn't resist playing along. "Oh, you bet! You're coming along for the ride, my friend, whether you like it or not! Hahahaha!" I added an animated evil grin emoji.

A playful banter ensued as we exchanged jabs, the excitement for future endeavors bubbling beneath the surface.

"Well, if you insist! But maybe we should wait a bit before initiating any company-wide changes," Bob suggested.

"Agreed. Oh, and by the way, I'm taking a much-needed vacation! So if you're up for it, feel free to kickstart the process in my absence. I'll be more than ready to lend a hand once I'm back. ;-)"

"Vacation?! Hold on, when exactly?" Bob's virtual eyes widened in playful disbelief.

I couldn't help but burst into laughter, a sense of giddiness washing over me. "Hehehehe."

With that, Bob and I shelved the topic for the moment. Who knew what insights I would garner during my time off or what ambitious projects Bob and I would set in motion upon my return. The future seemed ripe with endless possibilities.

CONCLUSION

AS WE BID FAREWELL to Wendy, Bob, and Peter, I hope their experiences have resonated with you. Though fictional, they are not just characters; they embody the challenges and triumphs many face in the modern workplace. Their journey goes beyond merely improving meetings; it represents a cultural shift in how organizations approach collaboration and communication, the cornerstone of success in today's work landscape.

Throughout this book, we've witnessed Wendy's efforts to transform the meeting mindset. She began by eliminating unnecessary meetings and teaching her colleagues to discern what truly requires face-to-face interaction. This crucial first step created the space needed to thoughtfully design and plan the necessary gatherings. It's a powerful reminder that meetings should be intentional, clearly designed, and well facilitated. They are purposeful tools for collaboration, not just default calendar fillers.

Their story offers practical strategies and serves as a road map for transformation. From their journey, we can extract several key lessons for organizations seeking to transform their collaboration approach:

- Embrace diverse collaboration methods beyond traditional meetings
- Leverage asynchronous communication to support deep work
- Prioritize psychological safety and meaningful human connection
- Cultivate a culture of experimentation where failure leads to learning
- Secure leadership buy-in to pilot and scale changes

An organization can move only at the speed of trust. Fostering a culture where people feel empowered to make decisions without constantly needing consensus from everyone is the foundation upon which these changes can be built and sustained.

In the spirit of revolutionizing our approach to meetings and work, let's carry forward the torch lit by Wendy, Bob, and Peter. As you step back into your own professional realm, armed with newfound strategies and perspectives, remember that the power to transform lies within each of us. The status quo won't change itself. Be the pioneer who leads the way.

With the blueprint now in hand, it's time for action. This is not about making sweeping changes overnight; after all, Rome wasn't built in a day. Psychological safety and trust, the foundations of any productive interaction, are established through consistent, small actions. Each meeting, each interaction, is another stone laid in this bedrock.

So start with baby steps. Even the smallest adjustments can spark profound shifts in workplace culture. Begin by implementing one new collaboration tactic with your team. Gather feedback and iterate. If you're unsure where to begin, revisit chapter 1 and try the exercise outlined there.

Lead by example. Seed the values of trust and flexibility through your words and actions. Let these principles guide your approach to fostering a more collaborative workplace culture. While Wendy's adventure may be ending, the journey toward a thriving, collaborative workplace is just beginning.

Finally, don't forget the importance of allies and support. Collaborate with leadership and colleagues to run pilot programs. Consider who you can partner with on this journey. If you're in senior leadership, do you have someone like Wendy or Bob who could join forces with you? How can you best support them? Could you be the executive champion driving this initiative across the entire company?

If you're not an executive, seek out someone in senior management who would champion your efforts. Having an executive advocate can significantly bolster your endeavors. Keep in mind that this champion doesn't need to be within your direct chain of command; sometimes support can come from unexpected places in the organization. The key is to find someone who shares your vision for a more collaborative workplace and has the influence to help make it a reality.

The path ahead is not a short one and it requires focus, courage, and creativity. You may encounter resistance from those accustomed to the old ways, but with persistence and compassion, you can model new ways of working and cultivate an environment where productivity and connection coexist harmoniously.

This evolution in our work culture is just the beginning. You have the power to drive meaningful change, transforming meetings from mere boxes on a calendar into stepping stones toward a more connected, innovative, and fulfilling professional life.

As we continue this journey, I challenge you to think beyond the traditional boundaries. If meetings are to be intentional, what does that mean for your team, especially if they are doing more asynchronous work and haven't interacted as often? Can or should your meetings serve multiple purposes—work, play, and relationship building? And if so, where should these meetings take place?

Consider the space and structure of your meetings. How can the flow of your meetings reflect these various purposes?

- In Person: Does the conference room in your office serve the needs of both productivity and connection? Perhaps it's time to rethink and repurpose your office space.

- Online: Is your current video conference tool able to support these needs?

To help you navigate these questions and design meetings that truly matter, I've created a checklist as a free gift just for you. This handy guide will walk you through a process of identifying your team's most pressing collaboration needs and show you the considerations that you'll need to take to ensure your meetings are intentional, impactful, and aligned with your team's needs, whether they're in person or online. Use the following URL to sign up to receive this free checklist and take the next step in your journey toward better collaboration and fewer meetings: https://munwaic.com/meeting-checklist/.

Thank you for joining me on this remarkable odyssey. The future of work depends on courageous individuals like you. I wish you the very best in your endeavors ahead. Now go and make your meetings matter!

NOTES

1. Chung, Mun-Wai. *How to Make a Case to Senior Management.* 14 February 2021. *MunWai Consulting*, https://munwaic. com/2021/02/14/how-to-make-a-case-to-senior-management/.

2. Hale, Justin. *Five Reasons Employees Hate Meetings and How Leaders Can Improve the Process.* 10 August 2022. *Forbes*, https:// www.forbes.com/councils/forbescoachescouncil/2022/08/10/ five-reasons-employees-hate-meetings-and-how-leaders-can- improve-the-process/.

3. *VARK Learning Styles*, https://vark-learn.com/.

4. *Modern Agile*, https://modernagile.org/.

ABOUT THE AUTHOR

MUN-WAI, a business agility consultant and executive coach, specializes in creating and maintaining innovative organizations. With over twenty years of corporate and agile experience, her career has spanned a variety of roles from engineering to senior management positions. Clients value her pragmatic and human-centric systems approach, which she applies to organizations worldwide, from start-ups to large enterprises across high-tech, hardware, telecommunications, cybersecurity, and pharmaceutical industries. Mun-Wai understands how top-level decisions impact global operations and how collaboration affects an organization's innovation and overall success.

A firm believer in the principle, "Release the potential of your staff and they will release the potential of the business," Mun-Wai is a sought-after speaker at global conferences and professional events. She also shares her insights through her podcast, blogs, articles, and monthly Leadership Memos at https://www.munwaic.com.

OG

www.ingramcontent.com/pod-product-compliance
Lightning Source LLC
Chambersburg PA
CBHW071429210326
41597CB00020B/3717